THE AUSTRALIAN
Women's Weekly

classic

CAKES

Sponges TEACAKES fruit cakes

THE AUSTRALIAN
Women's Weekly

classic

CAKES

Sponges TEACAKES *fruit cakes*

acp
books

Contents

introduction 6

Classic Butter Cakes 8
Classic Sponge Cakes 52
Classic Chocolate Cakes 84
Classic Fruit Cakes 108
Classic Syrup Cakes 164
Classic Dessert Cakes 188

EQUIPMENT 226 BAKING TECHNIQUES 228
GLOSSARY 234 CONVERSION CHART 236 INDEX 237

Introduction

CAKES

The Australian Women's Weekly Test Kitchen
has a reputation for producing wonderful
recipes of all types, but when it comes to
baking, we lead the field. The cakes in this
cookbook cover the spectrum, from the
simplest teacakes through to glamorous
dessert cakes, cakes for Christmas and just
about every other occasion. In fact, every
recipe you'd expect to find in a collection of
classics. The recipes are triple-tested, often
more, and photographed beautifully.

Dessert

Most cakes can double as a dessert. Serve a warm wedge of just about any cake you can think of – the microwave oven does a good job of this – dollop the cake with ice-cream, custard (think fruit cake turning into a pudding here), half milk and half pouring cream (great with a simple chocolate cake) or thick cream.

WHITE, MILK & DARK CHOCOLATE

Chocolate cakes – white, milk or dark – can be made by many different methods, the simplest method of all being melt and mix, where usually the whole process of making the mixture involves the use of just one bowl or saucepan and a spoon. The ever popular mud cakes are often made this way, simple to make and decadently rich to eat, this has to be a winning combination. The only tricky part to making cakes by this easy method is cooling the melted ingredients to the right temperature before the eggs and dry ingredients etc., are added to the mixture. We use a regular supermarket-bought eating quality chocolate in our recipes for consistently good results.

SPONGE CAKES

The sponge-making method involves lots of aeration. The key to success is getting the air into the mixture and holding it there before and during the baking. All sponge recipes involve beating air into the eggs. Some recipes tell you to beat the whole eggs, others just the egg whites, before adding the sugar. The whole egg method is easier, because the egg yolks, which include fat, make it almost impossible to over-beat the mixture, whereas the egg whites can easily be over-beaten, and then dry out, making it difficult to dissolve the sugar. Folding in flour and any other ingredients is where most beginner cooks come unstuck. If you're having trouble using a spatula, spoon or whisk for the folding-in process, try using your hand like a rake, pulling the flour etc., up and through the egg mixture. This works for me.

{ GLORIOUS CAKES }

Baking is fun and rewarding, and with a little practice you'll soon become an expert. Make notes to yourself about textures of mixtures, beating and baking times; these notes will help you remember and refine your techniques.

Butter and fruit cakes are first cousins

✱ Most butter and fruit cakes are made by the "creaming" method. This is an easy method if you have an electric mixer, especially a stand-alone mixer – you can be doing other things while the mixer gets on with the job. A hand-held mixer works just as well, but boredom is inclined to set in, so there is a tendency to underbeat the mixture, resulting in a less than perfect cake.

✱ The traditional method of creaming involved a lot of hard work, beating the butter, sugar and egg mixture either with your hand or with a wooden spoon. If you don't have an electric mixer, it's good to know that your hand will do a better, and quicker, job than a wooden spoon, simply because your hand is warm and will soften the butter more readily than the spoon Do it once just for the fun – and feel – of it.

Butter cakes

1

Most of the cakes we know and love are butter cakes of some sort. We use butter in our recipes because it will hold the flavour of the cake, it will keep the texture moist, and the cake will cut and keep well, but, best of all, it makes the cakes taste just wonderful.

basic butter cake

250g butter, softened
1 teaspoon vanilla extract
1¼ cups (275g) caster sugar
3 eggs
2¼ cups (335g) self-raising flour
¾ cup (180ml) milk

1 Preheat oven to 180°C/160°C fan-forced. Grease deep 22cm-round or 19cm-square cake pan; line base with baking paper. **2** Beat butter, extract and sugar in medium bowl with electric mixer until light and fluffy. Beat in eggs, one at a time. Stir in sifted flour and milk, in two batches.
3 Spread mixture into pan; bake about 1 hour. Stand cake in pan 5 minutes before turning, top-side up, onto wire rack to cool.

{ **prep + cook time** 1 hour 30 minutes **serves** 12 }

marble cake

250g butter, softened
1 teaspoon vanilla extract
1¼ cups (275g) caster sugar
3 eggs
2¼ cups (335g) self-raising flour
¾ cup (180ml) milk
pink food colouring
2 tablespoons cocoa powder
2 tablespoons milk, extra
BUTTER FROSTING
90g butter, softened
1 cup (160g) icing sugar
1 tablespoon milk

1 Preheat oven to 180°C/160°C fan-forced. Grease deep 22cm-round or 19cm-square cake pan; line base with baking paper.
2 Beat butter, extract and sugar in medium bowl with electric mixer until light and fluffy. Beat in eggs, one at a time. Stir in sifted flour and milk, in two batches.
3 Divide mixture among three bowls; tint one mixture pink. Blend sifted cocoa with extra milk in a cup; stir into second mixture; leave remaining mixture plain. Drop alternate spoonfuls of mixtures into pan. Pull a skewer backwards and forwards through cake mixture.
4 Bake cake about 1 hour. Stand cake in pan 5 minutes before turning, top-side up, onto wire rack to cool.
5 Make butter frosting. Spread frosting over top of cake.
BUTTER FROSTING Beat butter in small bowl with electric mixer until light and fluffy; beat in sifted icing sugar and milk, in two batches.

{**prep + cook time** 1 hour 40 minutes **serves** 12}

lemon sour cream cake

250g butter, softened
1 tablespoon finely grated lemon rind
2 cups (440g) caster sugar
6 eggs
¾ cup (180g) sour cream
2 cups (300g) plain flour
¼ cup (35g) self-raising flour
½ cup (80g) pine nuts
1 tablespoon demerara sugar
¼ cup (90g) honey

1 Preheat oven to 180°C/160°C fan-forced. Grease deep 23cm-square cake pan; line base and two opposite sides with baking paper, extending paper 5cm over edges.
2 Beat butter, rind and caster sugar in medium bowl with electric mixer until light and fluffy. Beat in eggs, one at a time. Stir in sour cream and sifted flours, in two batches. Spread mixture into pan; bake 15 minutes.
3 Meanwhile, combine pine nuts and demerara sugar in small bowl.

4 Remove cake from oven; working quickly, sprinkle nut mixture evenly over cake, press gently into top. Return cake to oven; bake a further 45 minutes. Stand cake in pan 5 minutes before turning, top-side up, onto wire rack.
5 Meanwhile, heat honey in small saucepan. Drizzle hot cake evenly with hot honey; cool before serving.

{**prep + cook time** 1 hour 15 minutes **serves** 16}

orange cake

150g butter, softened
1 tablespoon finely grated orange rind
⅔ cup (150g) caster sugar
3 eggs
1½ cups (225g) self-raising flour
¼ cup (60ml) milk
¾ cup (120g) icing sugar
1½ tablespoons orange juice

1 Preheat oven to 180°C/160°C fan-forced. Grease deep 20cm-round cake pan; line base with baking paper.
2 Beat butter, rind, caster sugar, eggs, flour and milk in medium bowl on low speed with electric mixer until just combined. Increase speed to medium; beat about 3 minutes or until mixture is smooth and pale in colour.

3 Spread mixture into pan; bake about 40 minutes. Stand cake in pan 5 minutes before turning, top-side up, onto wire rack to cool.
4 Meanwhile, combine sifted icing sugar and juice in small bowl; stir until smooth. Spread icing over cake.

{ **prep + cook time** 50 minutes **serves** 12 }

cut & keep butter cake

125g butter, softened
1 teaspoon vanilla extract
1¼ cups (275g) caster sugar
3 eggs
1 cup (150g) plain flour
½ cup (75g) self-raising flour
¼ teaspoon bicarbonate of soda
½ cup (125ml) milk

1 Preheat oven to 180°C/160°C fan-forced. Grease deep 20cm-round cake pan; line base with baking paper.
2 Beat ingredients in medium bowl on low speed with electric mixer until just combined. Increase speed to medium; beat about 3 minutes or until mixture is smooth and pale in colour.

3 Spread mixture into pan; bake about 1¼ hours. Stand cake in pan 5 minutes before turning, top-side up, onto wire rack to cool. Dust cake with sifted icing sugar, if desired.

{ **prep + cook time** 1 hour 30 minutes **serves** 10 }

madeira cake

180g butter, softened
2 teaspoons finely grated lemon rind
⅔ cup (150g) caster sugar
3 eggs
¾ cup (110g) plain flour
¾ cup (110g) self-raising flour
⅓ cup (55g) mixed peel
¼ cup (35g) slivered almonds

1 Preheat oven to 160°C/140°C fan-forced. Grease deep 20cm-round cake pan; line base with baking paper.
2 Beat butter, rind and sugar in small bowl with electric mixer until light and fluffy; beat in eggs, one at a time. Transfer mixture to large bowl, stir in sifted flours.

3 Spread mixture into pan; bake 20 minutes. Remove cake from oven; sprinkle with peel and nuts. Return to oven; bake about 40 minutes. Stand cake in pan 5 minutes before turning, top-side up, onto wire rack to cool.

{ **prep + cook time** 1 hour 15 minutes **serves** 12 }

cinnamon teacake

60g butter, softened
1 teaspoon vanilla extract
⅔ cup (150g) caster sugar
1 egg
1 cup (150g) self-raising flour
⅓ cup (80ml) milk
10g butter, extra, melted
1 teaspoon ground cinnamon
1 tablespoon caster sugar, extra

1 Preheat oven to 180°C/160°C fan-forced. Grease deep 20cm-round cake pan; line base with baking paper.
2 Beat butter, extract, sugar and egg in small bowl with electric mixer until light and fluffy. Stir in sifted flour and milk.
3 Spread mixture into pan; bake about 30 minutes. Stand cake in pan 5 minutes before turning, top-side up, onto wire rack. Brush top of cake with melted butter; sprinkle with combined cinnamon and extra sugar. Serve warm with whipped cream or butter.

{ **prep + cook time** 50 minutes **serves** 10 }

almond butter cake

250g butter, softened
1 teaspoon almond essence
1 cup (220g) caster sugar
4 eggs
1 cup (150g) self-raising flour
½ cup (75g) plain flour
¾ cup (90g) almond meal

1 Preheat oven to 180°C/160°C fan-forced. Grease deep 19cm-square cake pan; line base and two opposite sides with baking paper, extending paper 5cm over edges.
2 Beat butter, essence and sugar in medium bowl with electric mixer until light and fluffy. Beat in eggs, one at a time. Fold in sifted flours and almond meal in two batches.

3 Spread mixture into pan; bake for 30 minutes. Reduce oven temperature to 160°C/140°C fan-forced; bake a further 30 minutes. Stand cake in pan 5 minutes before turning, top-side up, onto wire rack to cool. Serve dusted with icing sugar and toasted flaked almonds, if you like.

{ **prep + cook time** 1 hour 20 minutes **serves** 10 }

gingerbread loaves

200g butter, softened
1¼ cups (275g) caster sugar
¾ cup (270g) treacle
2 eggs
3 cups (450g) plain flour
1½ tablespoons ground ginger
3 teaspoons mixed spice
1 teaspoon bicarbonate of soda
¾ cup (180ml) milk
VANILLA ICING
3 cups (480g) icing sugar
2 teaspoons butter, softened
½ teaspoon vanilla extract
⅓ cup (80ml) milk

1 Preheat oven to 180°C/160°C fan-forced. Grease two eight-hole (½-cup/125ml) petite loaf pans or line 22 holes of two 12-hole (⅓-cup/80ml) muffin pans with paper cases.
2 Beat butter and sugar in small bowl with electric mixer until light and fluffy. Pour in treacle; beat 3 minutes. Beat in eggs, one at a time. Transfer mixture to large bowl; stir in sifted dry ingredients, then milk.

3 Divide mixture among pans. Bake about 25 minutes. Stand cakes in pans 5 minutes before turning, top-sides up, onto wire rack to cool.
4 Meanwhile, make vanilla icing. Spread icing over loaves; stand until set.
VANILLA ICING Sift icing sugar into heatproof bowl; stir in butter, extract and milk to form a smooth paste. Place bowl over simmering water; stir until icing is a spreadable consistency.

{ **prep + cook time** 1 hour **makes** 16 or 22 }

greek yogurt cake

125g butter, softened
1 cup (220g) caster sugar
3 eggs, separated
2 cups (300g) self-raising flour
½ teaspoon bicarbonate of soda
¼ cup (40g) finely chopped blanched almonds
1 cup (280g) yogurt

1 Preheat oven to 180°C/160°C fan-forced. Grease 20cm x 30cm lamington pan; line base and long sides with baking paper, extending paper 5cm over edges.
2 Beat butter and sugar in small bowl with electric mixer until light and fluffy. Add egg yolks, beat well. Transfer mixture to large bowl; stir in sifted flour and soda in two batches, then nuts and yogurt.

3 Beat egg whites in small bowl with electric mixer until soft peaks form. Gently fold egg whites into yogurt mixture in two batches.
4 Spread mixture into pan; bake about 35 minutes. Stand cake in pan 5 minutes before turning, top-side up, onto wire rack to cool. Dust cake with sifted icing sugar, if desired.

{ **prep + cook time** 1 hour **serves** 12 }

english malt loaf

4 cups (640g) wholemeal plain flour
½ cup (110g) firmly packed brown sugar
1½ cups (250g) sultanas
1 teaspoon bicarbonate of soda
1 tablespoon hot water
1¼ cups (310ml) milk
1 cup (250ml) liquid malt
½ cup (125ml) treacle

1 Preheat oven to 160°C/140°C fan-forced. Grease 15cm x 25cm loaf pan; line base with baking paper.
2 Sift flour into large heatproof bowl; stir in sugar and sultanas.
3 Add soda to the water in medium jug; stir in milk.
4 Place malt and treacle in medium saucepan; stir over low heat until mixture begins to bubble; stir in milk mixture. Stir foaming milk mixture into flour mixture.
5 Spread mixture into prepared pan; bake about 1¾ hours. Stand cake in pan 5 minutes before turning, top-side up, onto wire rack to cool.

{ **prep + cook time** 2 hours **serves** 10 }

tip Liquid malt is a malt extract available from brewing shops and some health-food stores.

quick-mix patty cakes

125g butter, softened
½ teaspoon vanilla extract
¾ cup (165g) caster sugar
3 eggs
2 cups (300g) self-raising flour
¼ cup (60ml) milk

1 Preheat oven to 180°C/160°C fan-forced. Line two 12-hole (2 tablespoons/40ml) deep flat-based patty pans with paper cases.
2 Beat ingredients in medium bowl on low speed with electric mixer until ingredients are just combined. Increase speed to medium; beat about 3 minutes or until mixture is smooth and pale in colour.
3 Drop rounded tablespoons of mixture into paper cases; bake about 20 minutes. Stand cakes in pans 5 minutes before turning, top-sides up, onto wire racks to cool.
4 Top cakes with icing of your choice.

{ **prep + cook time** 40 minutes **makes** 24 }

Variations

CHOCOLATE & ORANGE Stir in 1 teaspoon finely grated orange rind and ½ cup (95g) dark Choc Bits at the end of step 2.

PASSIONFRUIT & LIME Stir in 1 teaspoon finely grated lime rind and ¼ cup (60ml) passionfruit pulp at the end of step 2.

BANANA & WHITE CHOCOLATE CHIP Stir in ½ cup overripe mashed banana and ½ cup (95g) white Choc Bits at the end of step 2.

MOCHA Blend 1 tablespoon sifted cocoa powder with 1 tablespoon strong black coffee; stir in at the end of step 2.

glacé icing

2 cups (320g) icing sugar
20g butter, melted
2 tablespoons hot water,
approximately

1 Place sifted icing sugar in small bowl; stir in butter and enough of the hot water to make a firm paste. Stir over small saucepan of simmering water until icing is spreadable.

Variations

CHOCOLATE Stir in 1 teaspoon sifted cocoa powder.

COFFEE Dissolve 1 teaspoon instant coffee granules in the hot water.

PASSIONFRUIT Stir in 1 tablespoon passionfruit pulp.

cherry almond cake

185g butter, softened
1 cup (220g) caster sugar
1 teaspoon almond essence
3 eggs
⅔ cup (140g) red glacé cherries, quartered
1 cup (160g) sultanas
⅔ cup (90g) slivered almonds
1 cup (150g) plain flour
½ cup (75g) self-raising flour
⅓ cup (80ml) milk

1 Preheat oven to 160°C/140°C fan-forced. Line base and side of deep 20cm-round cake pan with three thicknesses of baking paper, extending paper 5cm above edge.
2 Beat butter, sugar and essence in small bowl with electric mixer until light and fluffy. Beat in eggs, one at a time. Combine cherries, sultanas and nuts in large bowl; stir in butter mixture, sifted flours and milk.
3 Spread mixture into pan; bake about 1½ hours. Cover pan tightly with foil; cool cake in pan.

{ **prep + cook time** 1 hour 50 minutes (plus cooling time) **serves** 22 }

tip Cover cake loosely with foil during baking if it starts to overbrown. Give the cake quarter turns several times during baking to help it avoid browning unevenly.

butterfly cakes

125g butter, softened
1 teaspoon vanilla extract
⅔ cup (150g) caster sugar
3 eggs
1½ cups (225g) self-raising flour
¼ cup (60ml) milk
½ cup (160g) jam
300ml thickened cream, whipped

1 Preheat oven to 180°C/160°C fan-forced. Line two 12-hole (2 tablespoons/40ml) deep flat-based patty pans with paper cases.
2 Beat butter, extract, sugar, eggs, sifted flour and milk in small bowl on low speed with electric mixer until ingredients are just combined. Increase speed to medium; beat about 3 minutes or until mixture is smooth and pale in colour.
3 Drop slightly rounded tablespoons of mixture into paper cases. Bake about 20 minutes. Stand cakes in pans 5 minutes before turning, top-sides up, onto wire racks to cool.
4 Using sharp pointed vegetable knife, cut a circle from the top of each cake; cut circle in half to make two "wings". Fill cavities with jam and whipped cream. Place wings in position on top of cakes. Dust with a little sifted icing sugar before serving, if you like.

{**prep + cook time** 50 minutes **makes** 24}

upside-down cashew and maple syrup loaf

125g butter
¾ cup (150g) firmly packed brown sugar
2 eggs
1 cup (150g) self-raising flour
½ cup (75g) plain flour
½ teaspoon mixed spice
½ cup (120ml) sour cream
2 tablespoons pure maple syrup
90g butter, extra
½ cup (110g) firmly packed brown sugar, extra
2 tablespoons pure maple syrup, extra
1 cup (150g) unsalted roasted cashews, chopped coarsely

1 Preheat oven to 180°C/160°C fan-forced. Grease 15cm x 25cm loaf pan; line base and long sides with baking paper, extending paper 5cm above edges.
2 Beat butter, sugar, eggs, sifted flours and spice, cream and syrup in medium bowl on low speed with electric mixer until combined. Increase speed to medium; beat about 3 minutes or until mixture is smooth and pale in colour.

3 Beat extra butter, sugar and syrup in small bowl with wooden spoon until smooth; spread over base of pan. Sprinkle with cashews; spread with cake mixture. Bake about 1 hour. Stand cake in pan 5 minutes before turning out onto wire rack to cool.

{ **prep + cook time** 1 hour 20 minutes **serves** 10 }

ginger cake

1½ cups (330g) firmly packed brown sugar
1½ cups (225g) plain flour
1½ cups (225g) self-raising flour
½ teaspoon bicarbonate of soda
1 tablespoon ground ginger
2 teaspoons ground cinnamon
1 teaspoon ground nutmeg
250g butter, softened
2 eggs
1 cup (250ml) buttermilk
½ cup (175g) golden syrup
LEMON FROSTING
60g butter, softened
2 teaspoons finely grated lemon rind
2 tablespoons lemon juice
2 cups (320g) icing sugar

1 Preheat oven to 160°C/140°C fan-forced. Grease deep 23cm-square cake pan; line base with baking paper.
2 Sift dry ingredients into large bowl; add remaining ingredients. Beat mixture on low speed with electric mixer until ingredients are combined. Increase speed to medium; beat mixture about 3 minutes or until mixture is smooth and pale in colour.

3 Spread mixture into pan; bake about 1½ hours. Stand cake in pan 10 minutes before turning, top-side up, onto wire rack to cool.
4 Meanwhile, make lemon frosting. Spread cold cake with frosting.
LEMON FROSTING Using a wooden spoon, beat butter and rind in small bowl; gradually beat in juice and sifted icing sugar.

{**prep + cook time** 1 hour 45 minutes **serves** 24}

coconut cake

125g butter, softened
½ teaspoon coconut essence
1 cup (220g) caster sugar
2 eggs
½ cup (40g) desiccated coconut
1½ cups (225g) self-raising flour
1¼ cups (300g) sour cream
⅓ cup (80ml) milk
COCONUT ICE FROSTING
2 cups (320g) icing sugar
1⅓ cups (100g) desiccated coconut
2 egg whites, beaten lightly
pink food colouring

1 Preheat oven to 180°C/160°C fan-forced. Grease deep 23cm-square cake pan; line base with baking paper.
2 Beat butter, essence and sugar in small bowl with electric mixer until light and fluffy. Beat in eggs, one at a time. Transfer mixture to large bowl; stir in coconut, sifted flour, sour cream and milk, in two batches.
3 Spread mixture into pan; bake about 40 minutes. Stand cake in pan 5 minutes before turning, top-side up, onto wire rack to cool.
4 Meanwhile, make coconut ice frosting. Drop alternate spoonfuls of white and pink frosting onto cake; marble over top of cake.
COCONUT ICE FROSTING Sift icing sugar into medium bowl; stir in coconut and egg white. Place half the mixture in small bowl; tint with pink colouring.

{ **prep + cook time** 1 hour 5 minutes **serves** 20 }

kisses

125g butter, softened
½ cup (110g) caster sugar
1 egg
⅓ cup (50g) plain flour
¼ cup (35g) self-raising flour
⅔ cup (100g) cornflour
¼ cup (30g) custard powder
VIENNA CREAM
60g butter, softened
¾ cup (120g) icing sugar
2 teaspoons milk

1 Preheat oven to 180°C/160°C fan-forced. Grease two oven trays.
2 Beat butter and sugar in small bowl with electric mixer until smooth and creamy; beat in egg. Stir in sifted dry ingredients in two batches.
3 Spoon mixture into piping bag fitted with 1cm tube. Pipe 3cm-diameter rounds of mixture, about 3cm apart, onto trays. Bake about 10 minutes or until browned lightly. Loosen cakes; cool on trays.
4 Meanwhile, make vienna cream. Sandwich cold cakes with vienna cream; dust with a little extra sifted icing sugar, if desired.

VIENNA CREAM Beat butter until as white as possible. Gradually beat in half the sifted icing sugar; beat in milk. Gradually beat in remaining icing sugar.

{ **prep + cook time** 40 minutes **makes about** 40 }

cream cheese lemon cake

125g butter, chopped
125g cream cheese, chopped
3 teaspoons finely grated lemon rind
1 cup (220g) caster sugar
2 eggs
¾ cup (110g) self-raising flour
½ cup (75g) plain flour
GLACÉ ICING
1 cup (160g) icing sugar
10g butter, melted
2 tablespoons hot water approximately
½ teaspoon finely grated lemon rind

1 Preheat oven to 180°C/160°C fan-forced. Grease 20cm baba pan (or grease deep 20cm-round cake pan and line base and side with baking paper).
2 Beat ingredients in medium bowl on low speed with electric mixer until combined. Increase speed to medium; beat about 3 minutes or until mixture is smooth and pale in colour.

3 Spread mixture into pan; bake about 55 minutes. Stand cake in pan 5 minutes before turning onto wire rack to cool. Spoon icing over cold cake.
GLACÉ ICING Sift icing sugar into small heatproof bowl; stir in butter and enough of the water to make a firm paste. Stir over small saucepan of simmering water until icing is spreadable. Stir in rind.

{**prep + cook time** 1 hour 15 minutes **serves** 10}

pound cake

250g butter, softened
1 cup (220g) caster sugar
1 teaspoon vanilla extract
4 eggs
½ cup (75g) self-raising flour
1 cup (150g) plain flour

1 Preheat oven to 180°C/160°C fan-forced. Grease deep 20cm-round cake pan; line base with baking paper.
2 Beat butter, sugar and extract in small bowl with electric mixer until light and fluffy. Beat in eggs, one at a time. Transfer mixture to large bowl; fold in sifted flours in two batches.

3 Spread mixture into pan; bake about 1 hour. Stand cake in pan 5 minutes before turning, top-side up, onto wire rack to cool. If you like, serve with whipped cream and strawberries, and dust with sifted icing sugar.

{ **prep + cook time** 1 hour 20 minutes **serves** 12 }

coffee walnut streusel cake

1 tablespoon instant coffee granules
¼ cup (60ml) boiling water
125g butter, softened
1 cup (220g) caster sugar
1 teaspoon vanilla extract
2 eggs
⅔ cup (160g) sour cream
1¼ cups (185g) plain flour
¼ cup (35g) self-raising flour
¼ teaspoon bicarbonate of soda
WALNUT STREUSEL
⅔ cup (100g) self-raising flour
⅔ cup (150g) firmly packed brown sugar
100g cold butter, chopped
1 cup (110g) coarsely chopped walnuts, roasted

1 Preheat oven to 180°C/160°C fan-forced. Grease 20cm x 30cm lamington pan; line base and long sides with baking paper, extending paper 5cm over edges.
2 Combine coffee and the water in small bowl; stir until coffee dissolves. Cool 5 minutes.
3 Make walnut streusel.
4 Beat butter, sugar and extract in medium bowl with electric mixer until light and fluffy; beat in eggs, one at a time. Stir in sour cream and sifted flours and soda, in two batches. Stir in coffee mixture.
5 Spread mixture into pan; sprinkle walnut streusel over top of mixture. Sprinkle over remaining walnuts. Bake about 30 minutes.
WALNUT STREUSEL Combine flour and sugar in medium bowl; rub in butter, using fingertips, until mixture resembles coarse breadcrumbs. Stir in half the walnuts.

{**prep + cook time** 1 hour **serves** 12}

Sponge cakes

2

Eggs are the star ingredients in
sponge cakes, they are responsible
for the light airy textures and the
melt-in-the mouth appeal. A quick light
touch is needed when the other ingredients
are combined with the beaten egg mixture.
These cakes can be challenging to make,
but are worth the effort.

génoise sponge

4 eggs
½ cup (110g) caster sugar
⅔ cup (100g) plain flour
60g butter, melted, cooled
300ml thickened cream
1 tablespoon icing sugar
¼ cup (80g) strawberry jam, warmed
500g strawberries, sliced thinly
1 tablespoon icing sugar, extra

1 Preheat oven to 180°C/160°C fan-forced. Grease deep 20cm-round cake pan; line base with baking paper.
2 Combine eggs and sugar in large heatproof bowl, place over saucepan of simmering water (do not allow water to touch base of bowl); beat with electric mixer about 10 minutes or until mixture is thick and creamy. Remove bowl from saucepan; beat mixture until it returns to room temperature.
3 Sift half the flour over egg mixture; carefully fold in flour. Sift remaining flour into bowl, fold into mixture. Working quickly, fold in melted butter.

4 Pour mixture into pan; bake about 20 minutes. Turn immediately, top-side up, onto baking-paper-covered wire rack to cool.
5 Beat cream and sifted icing sugar in small bowl with electric mixer until soft peaks form. Split sponge in half; place one half, cut-side up, on serving plate. Spread with jam and cream; top with strawberries, then remaining sponge. Decorate cake with extra sifted icing sugar, and strawberries, if you like.

{ **prep + cook time** 1 hour **serves** 8 }

jam roll

3 eggs, separated
½ cup (110g) caster sugar
2 tablespoons hot milk
¾ cup (110g) self-raising flour
¼ cup (55g) caster sugar, extra
½ cup (160g) jam, warmed

1 Preheat oven to 200°C/180°C fan-forced. Grease 25cm x 30cm swiss roll pan; line base and long sides with baking paper, extending paper 5cm over sides.
2 Beat egg whites in small bowl with electric mixer until soft peaks form; gradually add sugar, 1 tablespoon at a time, beating until sugar is dissolved between additions. With motor operating, add egg yolks, one at a time, beating about 10 minutes or until mixture is thick and creamy.
3 Pour hot milk down side of bowl; add triple-sifted flour. Working quickly, use plastic spatula to fold milk and flour through egg mixture. Spread mixture into pan; bake about 8 minutes.
4 Meanwhile, place a piece of baking paper cut the same size as the pan on bench; sprinkle with extra sugar. Turn hot sponge onto paper; peel away lining paper. Cool; trim all sides of sponge.
5 Roll sponge from short side; unroll, spread evenly with jam. Re-roll cake, from same short side, by lifting paper and using it as a guide. Serve jam roll with whipped cream, if desired.

{**prep + cook time** 30 minutes **serves** 10}

ginger fluff roll

3 eggs
⅔ cup (150g) caster sugar
⅔ cup (100g) wheaten cornflour
1 teaspoon cream of tartar
½ teaspoon bicarbonate of soda
1 teaspoon cocoa powder
2 teaspoons ground ginger
½ teaspoon ground cinnamon
GINGER CREAM FILLING
¾ cup (180ml) thickened cream
2 tablespoons golden syrup
1 teaspoon ground ginger

1 Preheat oven to 180°C/160°C fan-forced. Grease 25cm x 30cm swiss roll pan; line base and long sides with baking paper, extending paper 5cm over sides.
2 Beat eggs and ½ cup of the sugar in small bowl with electric mixer until mixture is thick and creamy and sugar is dissolved.
3 Triple-sift dry ingredients; fold into egg mixture. Spread sponge mixture into pan; bake about 12 minutes.
4 Meanwhile, place a piece of baking paper cut the same size as the pan on bench; sprinkle with remaining sugar. Turn hot sponge onto paper; peel away lining paper. Cool; trim sides of sponge.
5 Meanwhile, make ginger cream filling.
6 Spread sponge with filling. Using paper as a guide, roll sponge from long side. Cover with plastic wrap; refrigerate 30 minutes.
GINGER CREAM FILLING Beat ingredients in small bowl with electric mixer until firm peaks form.

{**prep + cook time** 35 minutes (plus refrigeration time) **serves** 10}

featherlight sponge cake

4 eggs
¾ cup (165g) caster sugar
⅔ cup (100g) wheaten cornflour
¼ cup (30g) custard powder
1 teaspoon cream of tartar
½ teaspoon bicarbonate of soda
⅓ cup (110g) apricot jam
300ml thickened cream, whipped

1 Preheat oven to 180°C/160°C fan-forced. Grease and flour two deep 22cm-round cake pans; shake away excess flour.
2 Beat eggs and sugar in small bowl with electric mixer until mixture is thick and creamy and sugar is dissolved; transfer to large bowl.

3 Triple-sift dry ingredients; fold into egg mixture. Divide sponge mixture between pans; bake about 20 minutes. Turn sponges, top-side up, onto baking-paper-covered wire rack to cool.
4 Sandwich sponges with jam and cream.

{ **prep + cook time** 40 minutes **serves** 10 }

honey spice sponge cake

2 eggs
½ cup (110g) caster sugar
⅓ cup (50g) wheaten cornflour
1½ tablespoons custard powder
1 teaspoon mixed spice
½ teaspoon cream of tartar
¼ teaspoon bicarbonate of soda
300ml thickened cream
2 tablespoons honey
1 tablespoon icing sugar

1 Preheat oven to 180°C/160°C fan-forced. Grease 25cm x 30cm swiss roll pan; line base and long sides with baking paper, extending paper 5cm over sides.
2 Beat eggs and ⅓ cup of the sugar in small bowl with electric mixer about 10 minutes or until thick and creamy.
3 Meanwhile, triple-sift dry ingredients; fold into egg mixture. Spread mixture into pan; bake 10 minutes.
4 Place a piece of baking paper cut the same size as the pan on bench; sprinkle evenly with remaining sugar. Turn hot sponge onto paper; peel away lining paper. Cool; trim all sides of sponge.
5 Beat cream and honey in small bowl with electric mixer until firm peaks form.
6 Cut sponge widthways into three equal-sized rectangles. Place one piece of sponge on serving plate; spread with half the cream mixture. Top with second piece of sponge and remaining cream. Finish with remaining sponge piece then dust with sifted icing sugar.

{ **prep + cook time** 30 minutes **serves** 6 }

strawberry powder puffs

2 eggs
⅓ cup (75g) caster sugar
2 tablespoons cornflour
2 tablespoons plain flour
2 tablespoons self-raising flour
½ cup (125ml) thickened cream
2 tablespoons icing sugar
½ cup (65g) finely chopped strawberries

1 Preheat oven to 180°C/160°C fan-forced. Grease and flour three 12-hole shallow (1-tablespoon/20ml) round-based patty pans; shake away excess flour.
2 Beat eggs and sugar in small bowl with electric mixer about 4 minutes or until thick and creamy. Triple-sift flours; fold into egg mixture.
3 Drop 1 teaspoon of mixture into pan holes. Bake about 7 minutes; turn immediately onto wire racks to cool.
4 Beat cream and half the sifted icing sugar in small bowl with electric mixer until firm peaks form; fold in strawberries. Sandwich puffs with strawberry cream just before serving. Dust with remaining sifted icing sugar.

{**prep + cook time** 40 minutes **makes** 36}

tip If you don't have three patty pan trays, just wash, grease and flour the pan again, and continue using until all the mixture is baked.

strawberry jelly cakes

6 eggs
⅔ cup (150g) caster sugar
⅓ cup (50g) cornflour
½ cup (75g) plain flour
⅓ cup (50g) self-raising flour
80g packet strawberry jelly crystals
2 cups (160g) desiccated coconut
300ml thickened cream, whipped

1 Preheat oven to 180°C/160°C fan-forced. Grease 20cm x 30cm lamington pan; line base and long sides with baking paper, extending paper 5cm over sides.
2 Beat eggs in large bowl with electric mixer about 10 minutes or until thick and creamy; gradually add sugar, beating until dissolved between additions. Triple-sift flours; fold into egg mixture.
3 Spread mixture into pan; bake about 35 minutes. Turn cake immediately onto baking-paper-covered wire rack to cool.

4 Meanwhile, make jelly as per packet instructions; refrigerate until set to the consistency of unbeaten egg white.
5 Trim all sides of cake. Cut cake into 15 squares; dip squares into jelly, drain off excess. Place coconut into medium bowl; toss squares in coconut. Refrigerate 30 minutes. Halve cakes horizontally; sandwich cakes with whipped cream.

{ **prep + cook time** 50 minutes (plus refrigeration time) **makes** 15 }

lamingtons

6 eggs
⅔ cup (150g) caster sugar
⅓ cup (50g) cornflour
½ cup (75g) plain flour
⅓ cup (50g) self-raising flour
2 cups (160g) desiccated coconut
CHOCOLATE ICING
4 cups (640g) icing sugar
½ cup (50g) cocoa powder
15g butter, melted
1 cup (250ml) milk

1 Preheat oven to 180°C/160°C fan-forced. Grease 20cm x 30cm lamington pan; line base and long sides with baking paper, extending paper 5cm over sides.
2 Beat eggs in large bowl with electric mixer about 10 minutes or until thick and creamy; gradually add sugar, beating until dissolved between additions. Triple-sift flours; fold into egg mixture.
3 Spread mixture into pan; bake about 35 minutes. Turn cake immediately onto baking-paper-covered wire rack to cool.

4 Meanwhile, make chocolate icing.
5 Cut cake into 16 squares; dip each square into icing, drain off excess. Place coconut into medium bowl; toss squares in coconut. Place lamingtons on wire rack to set.
CHOCOLATE ICING Sift icing sugar and cocoa into medium heatproof bowl; stir in butter and milk. Set bowl over medium saucepan of simmering water; stir until icing is of a coating consistency.

{**prep + cook time** 50 minutes **makes** 16}

Victoria sponge sandwich

250g butter
1 teaspoon vanilla extract
1 cup (220g) caster sugar
4 eggs
⅓ cup (80ml) milk
2 cups (300g) self-raising flour
⅓ cup (110g) raspberry jam, warmed

1 Preheat oven to 180°C/160°C fan-forced. Grease two deep 20cm-round cake pans; line bases with baking paper.
2 Beat butter, extract and sugar in small bowl with electric mixer until light and fluffy. Beat in eggs, one at a time. Add milk and beat well. Transfer mixture to large bowl. Stir in half the sifted flour, then remaining sifted flour; stir until mixture is smooth.
3 Divide mixture evenly between pans; bake about 30 minutes.
4 Turn cakes, top-sides up, onto baking-paper-covered wire rack to cool. Sandwich cakes with jam; dust with sifted icing sugar, if you like.

{ **prep + cook time** 50 minutes **serves** 10 }

chocolate sponge

3 eggs
½ cup (110g) caster sugar
¼ cup (35g) cornflour
¼ cup (35g) plain flour
¼ cup (35g) self-raising flour
2 tablespoons cocoa powder
300ml thickened cream, whipped
COFFEE ICING
3 teaspoons instant coffee granules
2 tablespoons milk
1½ cups (240g) icing sugar
1 teaspoon softened butter

1 Preheat oven to 180°C/160°C fan-forced. Grease deep 22cm-round cake pan; line base with baking paper.
2 Beat eggs in small bowl with electric mixer about 10 minutes or until thick and creamy; gradually add sugar, beating until dissolved between additions; transfer mixture to large bowl. Triple-sift dry ingredients; fold into egg mixture.
3 Spread mixture into pan; bake about 25 minutes. Turn sponge immediately onto baking-paper-covered wire rack to cool.

4 Make coffee icing.
5 Split sponge in half; sandwich with cream. Spread top with coffee icing; stand until set before cutting.
COFFEE ICING Combine coffee and milk in small bowl; stir until dissolved. Sift icing sugar into small bowl; stir in butter and enough of the coffee mixture to give a firm paste. Stir over hot water until icing is spreadable; do not over-heat. Use immediately.

{ **prep + cook time** 40 minutes (plus standing time) **serves** 10 }

lamington roll

3 eggs
½ cup (110g) caster sugar
¾ cup (110g) self-raising flour
2 tablespoons hot milk
¾ cup (60g) desiccated coconut
BUTTER CREAM FILLING
90g unsalted butter, softened
1 teaspoon vanilla extract
1 cup (160g) icing sugar
1 tablespoon milk
CHOCOLATE ICING
1 cup (160g) icing sugar
¼ cup (25g) cocoa powder
1 teaspoon softened butter
2 tablespoons milk

1 Preheat oven to 180°C/160°C fan-forced. Grease 26cm x 32cm swiss roll pan; line base and long sides with baking paper, extending paper 5cm over sides.
2 Beat eggs in small bowl with electric mixer about 10 minutes or until thick and creamy; gradually add sugar, beating until dissolved between additions. Fold in sifted flour and milk, in two batches; pour into pan. Bake about 12 minutes.
3 Place a piece of baking paper cut the same size as the pan on bench; sprinkle evenly with a third of the coconut. Turn hot sponge onto paper; peel away lining paper. Using paper as a guide, loosely roll sponge from long side. Stand 2 minutes; unroll. Cool; trim all sides of sponge.
4 Make butter cream filling. Make chocolate icing.

5 Spread filling over sponge. Using paper as a guide, roll sponge from long side. Place on wire rack set over tray; pour icing over roll. Press remaining coconut onto roll; refrigerate 30 minutes or until set.
BUTTER CREAM FILLING Beat butter and extract in small bowl with electric mixer until pale and creamy. Gradually beat in sifted icing sugar and milk until light and fluffy.
CHOCOLATE ICING Sift icing sugar and cocoa into small heatproof bowl; stir in butter and milk. Place bowl over small pan of simmering water; stir until icing reaches a pouring consistency.

{**prep + cook time** 45 minutes (plus refrigeration time) **serves** 10}

passionfruit curd sponge cakes

3 eggs
½ cup (110g) caster sugar
¾ cup (110g) self-raising flour
20g butter
¼ cup (60ml) boiling water
PASSIONFRUIT CURD
⅓ cup (80ml) passionfruit pulp
½ cup (110g) caster sugar
2 eggs, beaten lightly
125g unsalted butter, chopped coarsely

1 Make passionfruit curd.
2 Preheat oven to 180°C/160°C fan-forced. Grease 12-hole (½-cup/125ml) oval friand pan; dust lightly with flour.
3 Beat eggs in small bowl with electric mixer about 10 minutes or until thick and creamy. Gradually add sugar, beating until dissolved between additions. Transfer mixture to a large bowl. Fold in sifted flour then combined butter and the boiling water.
4 Divide mixture among pan holes; bake about 12 minutes. Working quickly, loosen edges of cakes from pan using a small knife; turn immediately onto baking-paper-covered wire racks to cool.
5 Split cooled cakes in half. Spread cut-sides with curd; replace tops. Dust lightly with sifted icing sugar before serving, if you like.
PASSIONFRUIT CURD Combine ingredients in medium heatproof bowl; stir over pan of simmering water about 10 minutes or until mixture coats the back of a wooden spoon (do not let water touch base of bowl). Cover; refrigerate 3 hours.

{**prep + cook time** 40 minutes (plus refrigeration time) **makes** 12}

ginger sponge

5 eggs, separated
¾ cup (165g) caster sugar
1 tablespoon golden syrup
⅓ cup (50g) self-raising flour
⅓ cup (50g) cornflour
3 teaspoons ground ginger
1 teaspoon ground cinnamon
2 teaspoons cocoa powder
300ml thickened cream, whipped

1 Preheat oven to 180°C/160°C fan-forced. Grease two deep 20cm-round cake pans; line bases with baking paper.
2 Beat egg whites in medium bowl with electric mixer until soft peaks form; gradually add sugar, beating until sugar is dissolved between additions. Beat in egg yolks and golden syrup. Triple-sift dry ingredients; fold into egg mixture.

3 Pour mixture into pans; bake about 18 minutes. Immediately turn sponges, top-side up, onto baking-paper-covered wire rack to cool.
4 Sandwich sponges with whipped cream. Serve dusted with sifted icing sugar, if you like.

{**prep + cook time** 40 minutes **serves** 10}

best-ever sponge cake

4 eggs
¾ cup (165g) caster sugar
1 cup (150g) self-raising flour
1 tablespoon cornflour
10g butter, softened
⅓ cup (80ml) hot water
⅓ cup (115g) lemon butter
¾ cup (180ml) thickened cream, whipped
1 tablespoon icing sugar

1 Preheat oven to 180°C/160°C fan-forced. Grease two deep 20cm-round cake pans; line base with baking paper.
2 Beat eggs in small bowl with electric mixer about 10 minutes or until thick and creamy. Gradually add sugar, beating until dissolved between additions. Triple-sift flours; fold into egg mixture. Pour combined butter and the water down side of bowl; using one clean hand, fold through egg mixture.
3 Pour mixture evenly into pans; bake about 25 minutes. Immediately turn sponges, top-side up, onto baking-paper-covered wire rack to cool.
4 Sandwich sponges with lemon butter and cream. Serve dusted with sifted icing sugar.

{**prep + cook time** 50 minutes **serves** 8}

angel food cake

½ cup (75g) plain flour
½ cup (75g) wheaten cornflour
1¼ cups (275g) caster sugar
¼ teaspoon salt
12 egg whites
1 teaspoon cream of tartar
1 teaspoon vanilla extract

1 Preheat oven to 180°C/160°C fan-forced.
2 Sift flours, ¼ cup of the sugar and the salt together six times.
3 Beat egg whites in large bowl with electric mixer until foamy; beat in cream of tartar. Gradually add remaining sugar to egg mixture, beating until dissolved between additions. Add extract; beat until firm peaks form. Transfer egg mixture to a larger bowl; use a whisk to gently fold in flour mixture.
4 Spread mixture into ungreased 25cm tube pan; bake about 30 minutes.

5 Place a piece of baking paper cut larger than the pan on bench; turn pan upside down onto bench over baking paper (the pan should rest on its "feet", or the tube, above the paper) – do not move pan until cake is cold (the cake will drop from the pan when cold). If necessary, use a metal spatula to release the cold cake from the dome and base. Decorate with fresh berries, if you like.

{ **prep + cook time** 50 minutes (plus standing time) **serves** 10 }

tip A tube pan is a round cake pan with tall, smooth sides and a hollow metal tube in the centre. The tube (which may be higher than the outside of the pan) helps give a more even baking in the centre of the cake.

CLASSIC

Chocolate cakes

3

When in doubt about what kind of
cake to make, make it chocolate, you
won't go wrong. Chocolate cakes range in
density from extremely rich and moist like
mud cakes, flourless cakes and brownies
through to light, fluffy, spongy chiffon cakes
and everything in between.

mississippi mud cake

250g butter, chopped
150g dark eating chocolate, chopped
2 cups (440g) caster sugar
1 cup (250ml) hot water
⅓ cup (80ml) coffee liqueur
1 tablespoon instant coffee granules
1½ cups (225g) plain flour
¼ cup (35g) self-raising flour
¼ cup (25g) cocoa powder
2 eggs, beaten lightly
DARK CHOCOLATE GANACHE
½ cup (125ml) cream
200g dark eating chocolate, chopped coarsely

1 Preheat oven to 160°C/140°C fan-forced. Grease deep 20cm-round cake pan; line base and side with baking paper.
2 Combine butter, chocolate, sugar, the water, liqueur and coffee granules in medium saucepan. Using wooden spoon, stir over low heat until chocolate melts.
3 Transfer mixture to large bowl; cool 15 minutes. Whisk in combined sifted flours and cocoa, then egg. Pour mixture into prepared pan.

4 Bake cake about 1½ hours. Stand cake in pan 30 minutes before turning, top-side up, onto wire rack to cool.
5 Meanwhile, make dark chocolate ganache; spread over top of cake.
DARK CHOCOLATE GANACHE Bring cream to the boil in small saucepan. Pour hot cream over chocolate in medium heatproof bowl; stir until smooth. Stand at room temperature until spreadable.

{ **prep + cook time** 1 hour 45 minutes (plus cooling & standing time) **serves** 16 }

devil's food cake

180g butter, softened
1¾ cups (385g) caster sugar
3 eggs
1½ cups (225g) self-raising flour
½ cup (75g) plain flour
½ teaspoon bicarbonate of soda
⅔ cup (70g) cocoa powder
3 teaspoons instant coffee granules
½ cup (125ml) water
½ cup (125ml) milk
½ teaspoon red food colouring
300ml thickened cream, whipped
RICH CHOCOLATE FROSTING
60g dark eating chocolate, chopped
60g butter, chopped

1 Preheat oven to 180°C/160°C fan-forced. Grease two deep 20cm-round cake pans; line bases with baking paper.
2 Beat butter and sugar in small bowl with electric mixer until light and fluffy; beat in eggs, one at a time.
3 Transfer mixture to large bowl; fold in sifted flours, soda and cocoa powder with combined coffee, the water, milk and colouring, in two batches.
4 Pour mixture into pans; bake about 45 minutes. Stand cakes in pan 5 minutes before turning, top-side up, onto wire racks to cool.

5 Make rich chocolate frosting.
6 Sandwich cold cakes with whipped cream; top with frosting.
RICH CHOCOLATE FROSTING Combine chocolate and butter in small heatproof bowl over small saucepan of simmering water (water should not touch base of bowl); stir until smooth. Remove from heat. Cool at room temperature, stirring occasionally, until frosting is spreadable.

{ **prep + cook time** 1 hour **serves** 10 }

boiled chocolate cake

2 cups (500ml) water
3 cups (660g) caster sugar
250g butter, chopped
⅓ cup (35g) cocoa powder
1 teaspoon bicarbonate of soda
3 cups (450g) self-raising flour
4 eggs
FUDGE FROSTING
90g butter, chopped
⅓ cup (80ml) water
½ cup (110g) caster sugar
1½ cups (240g) icing sugar
⅓ cup (35g) cocoa powder

1 Preheat oven to 180°C/160°C fan-forced. Grease deep 26.5cm x 33cm, 3.5-litre (14-cup) baking dish; line base with baking paper.
2 Combine the water, sugar, butter and sifted cocoa and soda in medium saucepan; stir over heat, without boiling, until sugar dissolves. Bring to the boil then reduce heat; simmer, uncovered, 5 minutes. Transfer mixture to large bowl; cool to room temperature.
3 Add flour and eggs to bowl; beat with electric mixer until mixture is smooth and pale in colour. Pour mixture into pan; bake about 50 minutes. Stand cake in pan 10 minutes before turning, top-side up, onto wire rack to cool.
4 Meanwhile, make fudge frosting. Spread cold cake with frosting.
FUDGE FROSTING Combine butter, the water and caster sugar in small saucepan; stir over low heat, without boiling, until sugar dissolves. Sift icing sugar and cocoa into small bowl then gradually stir in hot butter mixture. Cover; refrigerate about 20 minutes or until frosting thickens. Beat with a wooden spoon until spreadable.

{ **prep + cook time** 1 hour 10 minutes (plus cooling time) **serves** 20 }

chocolate fudge brownies

150g butter, chopped
300g dark eating chocolate, chopped
1½ cups (330g) firmly packed brown sugar
3 eggs
1 teaspoon vanilla extract
¾ cup (110g) plain flour
¾ cup (140g) dark Choc Bits
½ cup (120g) sour cream
¾ cup (110g) roasted macadamias, chopped coarsely

1 Preheat oven to 180°C/160°C fan-forced. Grease 19cm x 29cm rectangular slice pan; line base and sides with baking paper, extending paper 5cm above long sides.
2 Combine butter and chocolate in medium saucepan; stir over low heat until smooth. Cool 10 minutes.
3 Stir in sugar, eggs and extract, then stir in sifted flour, Choc Bits, sour cream and nuts. Spread mixture into prepared pan; bake 40 minutes. Cover pan with foil; bake a further 20 minutes. Cool in pan before cutting into 16 pieces.
4 Dust brownies with sifted cocoa powder, if desired.

{ **prep + cook time** 1 hour 20 minutes **makes** 16 }

flourless chocolate hazelnut cake

⅓ cup (35g) cocoa powder
⅓ cup (80ml) hot water
150g dark eating chocolate, melted
150g butter, melted
1⅓ cups (295g) firmly packed brown sugar
1 cup (100g) hazelnut meal
4 eggs, separated
1 tablespoon cocoa powder, extra

1 Preheat oven to 180°C/160°C fan-forced. Grease deep 20cm-round cake pan; line base and side with baking paper.
2 Blend cocoa with the water in large bowl until smooth. Add chocolate, butter, sugar, hazelnut meal and egg yolks; stir until combined.

3 Beat egg whites in small bowl with electric mixer until soft peaks form; fold into chocolate mixture in two batches.
4 Pour mixture into pan; bake about 1 hour. Stand cake in pan 15 minutes before turning, top-side up, onto wire rack to cool. Dust with sifted extra cocoa.

{ **prep + cook time** 1 hour 30 minutes **serves** 8 }

one-bowl chocolate cake

125g butter, softened
1 teaspoon vanilla extract
1¼ cups (275g) caster sugar
2 eggs
1⅓ cups (200g) self-raising flour
½ cup (50g) cocoa powder
⅔ cup (160ml) water
CHOCOLATE ICING
90g dark eating chocolate, chopped coarsely
30g butter, softened
1 cup (160g) icing sugar
2 tablespoons hot water

1 Preheat oven to 180°C/160°C fan-forced. Grease deep 20cm-round cake pan; line with baking paper.
2 Beat butter, extract, sugar, eggs, sifted flour and cocoa, and the water in large bowl with electric mixer on low speed until ingredients are combined. Increase speed to medium; beat about 3 minutes or until mixture is smooth and pale in colour.
3 Spread mixture into pan; bake about 1 hour. Stand cake in pan 5 minutes before turning, top-side up, onto wire rack to cool.
4 Meanwhile, make chocolate icing. Spread cold cake with icing.
CHOCOLATE ICING Melt chocolate and butter in small heatproof bowl over small saucepan of simmering water (do not allow water to touch base of bowl); gradually stir in sifted icing sugar and the water, stirring until icing is spreadable.

{ **prep + cook time** 1 hour 20 minutes **serves** 10 }

sacher torte

150g dark eating chocolate, chopped
1 tablespoon water
150g butter, softened
½ cup (110g) caster sugar
3 eggs, separated
1 cup (150g) plain flour
2 tablespoons caster sugar, extra
1 cup (320g) apricot jam, warmed, strained
CHOCOLATE ICING
125g dark eating chocolate, chopped
125g butter, softened

1 Preheat oven to 180°C/160°C fan-forced. Grease deep 22cm-round cake pan; line base with baking paper.
2 Melt chocolate in small heatproof bowl over small saucepan of simmering water (do not allow water to touch base of bowl); stir in the water; cool mixture to room temperature.
3 Cream butter and sugar in small bowl with electric mixer until light and fluffy. Add egg yolks one at a time, beating until combined. Transfer mixture to large bowl; stir in chocolate mixture, then sifted flour.
4 Beat egg whites in small bowl until soft peaks form, gradually beat in extra sugar, beating until dissolved between each addition; fold into chocolate mixture.
5 Spread mixture into pan. Bake about 30 minutes. Stand cake in pan 5 minutes before turning onto wire rack to cool; leave cake upside down.
6 Meanwhile, make chocolate icing.
7 Split cold cake in half; place one half, cut-side up, on serving plate. Brush half the warmed jam over cake half, top with remaining cake half. Brush cake all over with remaining jam. Stand about 1 hour at room temperature or until jam has set. Spread top and side of cake with icing; stand at room temperature until icing has set. Serve with berries, if you like.
CHOCOLATE ICING Melt chocolate and butter in small heatproof bowl over small saucepan of simmering water (do not allow water to touch base of bowl). Cool at room temperature until spreadable, stirring occasionally; this can take up to 2 hours.

{ **prep + cook time** 1 hour 10 minutes (plus cooling & standing time) **serves** 10 }

tip This icing is also suitable for piping.

chocolate buttermilk cake

180g butter, softened
1 teaspoon vanilla extract
1½ cups (330g) caster sugar
4 eggs, separated
¾ cup (110g) self-raising flour
⅓ cup (35g) cocoa powder
¾ cup (180ml) buttermilk
CHOCOLATE FILLING
400g dark eating chocolate, melted
250g butter, melted
½ cup (80g) icing sugar

1 Preheat oven to 180°C/160°C fan-forced. Grease deep 20cm-round cake pan; line base with baking paper.
2 Beat butter, extract and sugar in small bowl with electric mixer until light and fluffy; beat in egg yolks, one at a time, until just combined. Transfer mixture to large bowl; stir in sifted dry ingredients and buttermilk.
3 Beat egg whites in clean small bowl with electric mixer until soft peaks form; fold into cake mixture in two batches. Pour mixture into pan. Bake about 1 hour. Cool cake in pan.

4 Meanwhile, make chocolate filling. Reserve about 1 cup of filling.
5 Split cake into three layers; place one layer on serving plate, spread thinly with some of the chocolate filling. Repeat layering with remaining cake layers and filling. Spread reserved filling all over cake. Refrigerate 3 hours before serving.
CHOCOLATE FILLING Combine chocolate and butter in medium bowl; stir in sifted icing sugar. Cool filling to room temperature; beat with wooden spoon until thick and spreadable.

{**prep + cook time** 1 hour 20 minutes (plus refrigeration time) **serves** 10}

chocolate fudge cake

250g dark eating chocolate, chopped
125g butter, chopped
⅔ cup (150g) caster sugar
⅔ cup (100g) self-raising flour
4 eggs, beaten lightly

1 Preheat oven to 180°C/160°C fan-forced. Grease 19cm x 29cm lamington pan; line base and long sides with baking paper, extending paper 5cm above sides.
2 Stir chocolate and butter in medium heatproof bowl over medium saucepan of simmering water (do not allow the water to touch base of bowl); cool.
3 Combine chocolate mixture and remaining ingredients in medium bowl; beat on low speed with electric mixer until ingredients are combined. Increase speed to medium; beat about 3 minutes or until mixture is changed in colour and smooth.
4 Pour mixture into pan; bake about 30 minutes. Stand cake 5 minutes before turning, top-side up, onto wire rack to cool. Serve dusted with sifted cocoa powder, if desired.

{**prep + cook time** 50 minutes **serves** 12}

chocolate chiffon cake

½ cup (50g) cocoa powder
¾ cup (180ml) boiling water
2 cups (300g) self-raising flour
1½ cups (330g) caster sugar
7 eggs, separated
½ cup (125ml) vegetable oil
1 teaspoon vanilla extract
WALNUT PRALINE
1 cup (220g) caster sugar
½ cup (50g) walnuts
60g dark eating chocolate, chopped
BRANDIED BUTTER CREAM
190g butter, softened
3 cups (480g) icing sugar
¼ cup (25g) cocoa powder
¼ cup (60ml) brandy

1 Preheat oven to 180°C/160°C fan-forced. Grease deep 22cm-round cake pan; cover base and side with baking paper.
2 Blend cocoa with the water in small bowl; cool. Sift flour and sugar into large bowl; add cocoa mixture, egg yolks, oil and extract. Beat with electric mixer until smooth and mixture is changed in colour.
3 Beat egg whites in large bowl with electric mixer until soft peaks form; fold into cocoa mixture in four batches.
4 Pour mixture into pan; bake about 1 hour or until firm. Stand cake 5 minutes before turning, top-side up, onto wire rack to cool.
5 Make walnut praline; make brandied butter cream.

6 Split cold cake into three layers; join layers with some of the butter cream. Spread cake evenly with remaining butter cream. Decorate with walnut praline.
WALNUT PRALINE Place sugar in heavy-based frying pan; cook over heat, without stirring, until sugar is melted and golden brown. Add nuts; pour onto greased oven tray; cool. Blend or process praline with chocolate until finely chopped.
BRANDIED BUTTER CREAM Cream butter in small bowl with electric mixer until as white as possible; beat in sifted icing sugar and cocoa, then brandy.

{ **prep + cook time** 1 hour 30 minutes **serves** 16 }

fudge-frosted chocolate cup cakes

2 cups (500ml) hot water
¾ cup (75g) cocoa powder, sifted
250g butter, softened
2 cups (440g) caster sugar
2 teaspoons vanilla extract
3 eggs
1½ cups (225g) plain flour
1 cup (150g) self-raising flour
½ teaspoon bicarbonate of soda
silver cachous
FUDGE FROSTING
50g butter, softened
¼ cup (60ml) milk
1 teaspoon vanilla extract
¼ cup (25g) cocoa powder
2 cups (320g) icing sugar

1 Preheat oven to 180°C/160°C fan-forced. Line two 12-hole (¹/₃-cup/80ml) muffin pans with paper cases.
2 Whisk the water and cocoa together in medium bowl.
3 Beat butter, sugar and vanilla in large bowl with electric mixer until light and fluffy. Beat in eggs, one at a time. Fold in half of the combined sifted flours and soda then half of the cocoa mixture; stir in remaining flour mixture and cocoa mixture until just combined.
4 Divide mixture among paper cases; bake about 25 minutes. Cool cakes in pans 5 minutes before turning onto wire racks to cool.
5 Meanwhile, make fudge frosting. Spread frosting over cakes; decorate with cachous.
FUDGE FROSTING Beat butter in medium bowl with electric mixer until light and fluffy. Add milk, extract, sifted cocoa and half the sifted icing sugar; beat about 5 minutes or until light and fluffy. Add remaining sifted icing sugar; beat a further 5 minutes.

{ **prep + cook time** 1 hour 10 minutes **makes** 24 }

CLASSIC

Fruit cakes

4

Fruit—dried, fresh, frozen or canned, along with some vegetables like carrot and zucchini, all go to make up ever-popular fruit cakes. The more fruit-packed the cakes are, the better they will keep. Store them airtight in a cool dark cupboard, or, if the weather is steamy, in the refrigerator.

banana cake

You will need 2 large (460g) overripe bananas to get the amount of mashed banana needed for this recipe.

125g butter, softened
¾ cup (165g) caster sugar
2 eggs
1 cup mashed banana
1 teaspoon bicarbonate of soda
2 tablespoons hot milk
1 cup (150g) plain flour
⅔ cup (100g) self-raising flour
icing sugar, to dust

1 Preheat oven to 180°C/160°C. Grease deep 20cm-round cake pan; line base and side with baking paper.
2 Beat butter and sugar in small bowl with electric mixer until light and fluffy. Beat in eggs, one at a time. Transfer to large bowl; stir in banana. Combine soda and milk in small jug; stir into banana mixture then stir in sifted flours.
3 Spread mixture into pan; bake about 50 minutes. Stand cake in pan 5 minutes before turning, top-side up, onto wire rack to cool. Dust with sifted icing sugar to serve.

{ **prep + cook time** 1 hour 15 minutes **serves** 10 }

banana cake
with passionfruit icing

You need two large overripe bananas (460g) and
two large passionfruit for this recipe.

125g butter, softened
¾ cup (165g) firmly packed brown sugar
2 eggs
1½ cups (225g) self-raising flour
½ teaspoon bicarbonate of soda
1 teaspoon mixed spice
1 cup mashed banana
½ cup (120g) sour cream
¼ cup (60ml) milk
PASSIONFRUIT ICING
1½ cups (240g) icing sugar
1 teaspoon soft butter
2 tablespoons passionfruit pulp, approximately

1 Preheat oven to 180°C/160°C fan-forced. Grease 15cm x 25cm loaf pan; line base with baking paper.
2 Beat butter and sugar in small bowl with electric mixer until light and fluffy. Beat in eggs, one at a time. Transfer to large bowl; stir in sifted dry ingredients, banana, sour cream and milk.

3 Spread mixture into pan; bake about 50 minutes. Stand cake in pan 5 minutes before turning, top-side up, onto wire rack to cool.
4 Meanwhile, make passionfruit icing. Spread cake with icing.
PASSIONFRUIT ICING Combine ingredients in medium bowl; stir until smooth.

{**prep + cook time** 1 hour 25 minutes **serves** 10}

boiled whisky fruit cake

1½ cups (220g) raisins
1½ cups (210g) dried seeded dates
1½ cups (250g) seeded prunes
1½ cups (250g) sultanas
⅓ cup (70g) red glacé cherries, quartered
⅓ cup (55g) mixed peel
2 tablespoons caster sugar
30g butter
½ cup (125ml) whisky
250g butter, chopped, extra
1 cup (220g) firmly packed dark brown sugar
½ teaspoon bicarbonate of soda
½ cup (70g) slivered almonds
2 cups (300g) plain flour
2 teaspoons mixed spice
5 eggs
¼ cup (60ml) whisky, extra

1 Chop raisins, dates and prunes the same size as the sultanas; combine in large bowl with sultanas, cherries and mixed peel.

2 Place caster sugar in large heavy-based saucepan over medium heat; move pan occasionally until sugar is melted. Add butter and whisky to pan; stir over low heat until smooth.

3 Add extra butter, brown sugar and fruit to pan. Stir over heat until butter melts; bring to the boil. Remove from heat; stir in soda. Transfer to large bowl, cover; stand overnight at room temperature.

4 Preheat oven to 150°C/130°C fan-forced. Grease deep 19cm-square cake pan; line base and sides with two layers of brown paper then baking paper, extending paper 5cm over edges.

5 Add nuts, sifted flour and spice, and eggs to fruit mixture; stir until combined.

6 Spoon mixture into corners of pan then spread remaining mixture into pan. Drop pan from a height of about 15cm onto bench to settle mixture into pan and to break any large air bubbles; level surface of cake with wet spatula. Bake about 3 hours.

7 Brush hot cake with extra whisky. Cover hot cake tightly with foil; cool in pan.

{ **prep + cook time** 3 hours 35 minutes (plus standing and cooling time) **serves** 16 }

sticky date cake with butterscotch sauce

3¾ cups (525g) dried pitted dates
3 cups (750ml) hot water
2 teaspoons bicarbonate of soda
185g butter, softened
2¼ cups (500g) firmly packed brown sugar
6 eggs
3 cups (450g) self-raising flour
½ cup (60g) coarsely chopped walnuts
½ cup (60g) coarsely chopped pecans
BUTTERSCOTCH SAUCE
2 cups (440g) firmly packed brown sugar
500ml thickened cream
250g butter, chopped

1 Preheat oven to 180°C/160°C fan-forced. Grease 26cm x 36cm baking dish; line base and long sides of dish with two layers baking paper, extending paper 5cm above edges.
2 Combine dates and the water in medium saucepan; bring to the boil. Remove from heat; stir in soda. Stand 5 minutes then blend or process date mixture until smooth.
3 Beat butter and sugar in large bowl with electric mixer until light and fluffy. Beat in eggs, one at a time. Stir date mixture and sifted flour into egg mixture; spread mixture into dish. Sprinkle with nuts; bake about 50 minutes. Stand cake in dish 10 minutes before turning, top-side up, onto wire rack to cool.
4 Meanwhile, make butterscotch sauce.
5 Brush surface of hot cake with ⅓ cup of the hot butterscotch sauce. Serve with remaining sauce.
BUTTERSCOTCH SAUCE Stir ingredients in medium saucepan over heat, without boiling, until sugar dissolves; bring to the boil. Reduce heat; simmer 3 minutes.

{**prep + cook time** 1 hour 10 minutes **serves** 20}

apple streusel cake

200g butter, softened
2 teaspoons finely grated lemon rind
⅔ cup (150g) caster sugar
3 eggs
1 cup (150g) self-raising flour
½ cup (75g) plain flour
⅓ cup (80ml) milk
5 medium apples (750g)
25g butter, extra
⅓ cup (75g) firmly packed brown sugar
STREUSEL
½ cup (75g) plain flour
¼ cup (35g) self-raising flour
⅓ cup (75g) firmly packed brown sugar
½ teaspoon ground cinnamon
80g cold butter, chopped finely

1 Preheat oven to 180°C/160°C fan-forced. Grease deep 23cm-round cake pan; line base with baking paper.
2 Make streusel.
3 Beat butter, rind and caster sugar in small bowl with electric mixer until light and fluffy. Beat in eggs, one at a time. Transfer to large bowl; stir in sifted flours and milk, in two batches. Spread mixture into pan; bake 25 minutes.
4 Meanwhile, peel, core and quarter apples; slice thinly. Melt extra butter in large frying pan, add apple; cook, stirring, about 5 minutes or until browned lightly. Add brown sugar; cook, stirring, about 5 minutes or until mixture thickens slightly. Set aside.
5 Remove cake from oven. Working quickly, top cake with apple mixture; coarsely grate streusel over apple. Return to oven; bake about 25 minutes. Stand cake in pan 10 minutes before turning, top-side up, onto wire rack to cool. Serve cake warm or cold.
STREUSEL Process flours, sugar and cinnamon until combined. Add butter; process until ingredients just come together. Wrap in plastic wrap; freeze about 1 hour or until firm.

{ **prep + cook time** 1 hour 15 minutes (plus freezing time) **serves** 16 }

hummingbird cake

You need two large overripe (460g) bananas for this recipe.

450g can crushed pineapple in syrup
1 cup (150g) plain flour
½ cup (75g) self-raising flour
½ teaspoon bicarbonate of soda
½ teaspoon ground cinnamon
½ teaspoon ground ginger
1 cup (220g) firmly packed brown sugar
½ cup (40g) desiccated coconut
1 cup mashed banana
2 eggs, beaten lightly
¾ cup (180ml) vegetable oil
CREAM CHEESE FROSTING
30g butter, softened
60g cream cheese, softened
1 teaspoon vanilla extract
1½ cups (240g) icing sugar

1 Preheat oven to 180°C/160°C fan-forced. Grease deep 23cm-square cake pan; line base with baking paper.
2 Drain pineapple over medium bowl, pressing with spoon to extract as much syrup as possible. Reserve ¼ cup (60ml) of the syrup.
3 Sift flours, soda, spices and sugar into large bowl. Using wooden spoon, stir in the drained pineapple, reserved syrup, coconut, banana, egg and oil.

4 Pour mixture into pan; bake about 40 minutes. Stand cake in pan 5 minutes before turning, top-side up, onto wire rack to cool.
5 Meanwhile, make cream cheese frosting; spread cake with frosting.
CREAM CHEESE FROSTING Beat butter, cream cheese and extract in small bowl with electric mixer until light and fluffy; gradually beat in sifted icing sugar.

{**prep + cook time** 1 hour 10 minutes **serves** 12}

lumberjack cake

2 large apples (400g), peeled, cored, chopped finely
1 cup (150g) finely chopped seeded dried dates
1 teaspoon bicarbonate of soda
1 cup (250ml) boiling water
125g butter, softened
1 teaspoon vanilla extract
1 cup (220g) caster sugar
1 egg
1½ cups (225g) plain flour
COCONUT TOPPING
60g butter, chopped
½ cup (110g) firmly packed brown sugar
½ cup (125ml) milk
⅔ cup (50g) shredded coconut

1 Preheat oven to 180°C/160°C fan-forced. Grease deep 23cm-square cake pan; line base and sides with baking paper.
2 Combine apple, dates and soda in large bowl, stir in the water; cover bowl with plastic wrap, stand 10 minutes.
3 Meanwhile, beat butter, extract, sugar and egg in small bowl with electric mixer until light and fluffy. Add butter mixture to apple mixture; stir to combine. Add sifted flour; stir to combine. Pour mixture into pan; bake about 50 minutes.
4 Meanwhile, make coconut topping.

5 Remove cake carefully from oven to bench. Using metal spatula, carefully spread warm topping evenly over cake; return to oven, bake about 20 minutes or until topping is browned.
6 Stand cake in pan 5 minutes before turning, top-side up, onto wire rack to cool.
COCONUT TOPPING Combine ingredients in medium saucepan; using wooden spoon, stir mixture over low heat until butter melts and sugar dissolves.

{ **prep + cook time** 1 hour 40 minutes **serves** 12 }

moist whole orange cake

2 medium oranges (480g)
⅔ cup (110g) blanched almonds, roasted
1 cup (220g) caster sugar
1 teaspoon baking powder
6 eggs
2 cups (250g) almond meal
2 tablespoons plain flour

1 Place unpeeled oranges in medium saucepan; cover with cold water, bring to the boil. Boil, covered, 30 minutes; drain. Repeat process with fresh water, boil about 1 hour or until oranges are tender; cool.
2 Preheat oven to 180°C/160°C fan-forced. Grease deep 22cm-round cake pan; line base and side with baking paper.
3 Process blanched almonds with 2 tablespoons of the sugar until finely chopped.
4 Trim ends off oranges and discard. Halve oranges; remove and discard seeds. Process oranges, including rind, with baking powder until mixture is pulpy.
5 Beat eggs and remaining sugar in medium bowl with electric mixer about 3 minutes or until fluffy and pale in colour. Fold in almond mixture, almond meal, sifted flour and orange pulp.
6 Pour mixture into pan; bake about 1 hour. Cool in pan.
7 Turn cake onto serving plate and dust with sifted icing sugar, if desired.

{**prep + cook time** 3 hours 10 minutes (plus cooling time) **serves** 10}

pecan and raisin loaf

⅓ cup (50g) raisins
90g butter, chopped
½ cup (110g) firmly packed brown sugar
⅓ cup (80ml) water
½ teaspoon bicarbonate of soda
2 eggs, beaten lightly
½ cup (60g) coarsely chopped pecans
½ cup (75g) plain flour
½ cup (75g) self-raising flour

1 Combine raisins, butter, sugar and the water in medium saucepan; bring to the boil. Remove from heat; stir in soda. Transfer mixture to medium bowl; cool 15 minutes.
2 Preheat oven to 150°C/130°C fan-forced. Grease 8cm x 25cm bar cake pan; line base with baking paper.

3 Stir egg and nuts into raisin mixture; stir in sifted flours. Pour mixture into pan; bake about 35 minutes. Stand cake in pan 5 minutes before turning, top-side up, onto wire rack to cool.

{**prep + cook time** 45 minutes (plus cooling time) **serves** 8}

date and walnut rolls

60g butter, chopped
1 cup (250ml) boiling water
1 cup (150g) finely chopped seeded dried dates
½ teaspoon bicarbonate of soda
1 cup (220g) firmly packed brown sugar
2 cups (300g) self-raising flour
½ cup (60g) coarsely chopped walnuts
1 egg, beaten lightly

1 Adjust oven shelves to fit upright tins.
2 Preheat oven to 180°C/160°C fan-forced. Grease two 8cm x 19cm nut roll tins; line bases with baking paper. Place tins upright on oven tray.
3 Combine butter and the water in medium saucepan; stir over low heat until butter melts.
4 Transfer mixture to large bowl; stir in dates and soda, then sugar, sifted flour, nuts and egg.
5 Spoon mixture into tins; replace lids. Bake rolls, tins standing upright, about 50 minutes.
6 Stand rolls 5 minutes, remove ends (top and bottom); shake tins gently to release nut rolls onto wire rack to cool.

{**prep + cook time** 1 hour 10 minutes **serves** 20}

yogurt fruit loaf

100g butter, softened
2 teaspoons finely grated orange rind
¾ cup (165g) caster sugar
2 eggs
2 cups (320g) wholemeal self-raising flour
1 cup (280g) yogurt
⅓ cup (80ml) orange juice
1 cup (200g) finely chopped dried figs
1 cup (160g) coarsely chopped raisins

1 Preheat oven to 180°C/160°C fan-forced. Grease 14cm x 21cm loaf pan.
2 Beat butter, rind, sugar, eggs, sifted flour, yogurt and juice in medium bowl with electric mixer, on low speed, until just combined. Stir in figs and raisins.

3 Pour mixture into pan; cover with foil. Bake 1¼ hours; remove foil, bake about 15 minutes. Stand loaf in pan 10 minutes before turning, top-side up, onto wire rack to cool. Serve at room temperature, or toasted, with butter.

{ **prep + cook time** 2 hours **serves** 10 }

one – bowl sultana loaf

125g butter, melted
750g sultanas
½ cup (110g) firmly packed brown sugar
2 tablespoons marmalade
2 eggs, lightly beaten
¼ cup (60ml) sweet sherry
¾ cup (110g) plain flour
¼ cup (35g) self-raising flour
30g blanched almonds
2 tablespoons apricot jam

1 Preheat oven to 150°C/130°C fan-forced. Grease 15cm x 25cm loaf pan; line base with baking paper.
2 Beat butter, sultanas, sugar, marmalade, egg, sherry and flours in large bowl using a wooden spoon until combined.

3 Spread mixture into pan; decorate top with blanched almonds. Bake about 1½ hours. Cover cake with foil; cool in pan. Brush cold cake with warmed sieved apricot jam.

{**prep + cook time** 1 hour 45 minutes **serves** 8}

apple custard tea cakes

90g butter, softened
½ teaspoon vanilla extract
½ cup (110g) caster sugar
2 eggs
¾ cup (110g) self-raising flour
¼ cup (30g) custard powder
2 tablespoons milk
1 unpeeled large apple (200g), cored, sliced finely
30g butter, extra, melted
1 tablespoon caster sugar, extra
½ teaspoon ground cinnamon
CUSTARD FILLING
1 tablespoon custard powder
1 tablespoon caster sugar
½ cup (125ml) milk
¼ teaspoon vanilla extract

1 Make custard filling.
2 Preheat oven to 180°C/160°C fan-forced. Line 12-hole (⅓-cup/80ml) muffin pan with paper cases.
3 Beat butter, extract, sugar, eggs, sifted flour and custard powder, and milk in small bowl with electric mixer, on low speed, until ingredients are just combined. Increase speed to medium, beat until mixture is pale in colour.
4 Divide half the mixture among paper cases; top with custard, then remaining cake mixture, spread mixture to cover custard. Top with apple, pressing slightly into cakes. Bake about 30 minutes.
5 Turn cakes, top-side up, onto wire rack. Brush hot cakes with extra butter, then sprinkle with combined extra sugar and cinnamon. Serve warm or cold.
CUSTARD FILLING Blend custard powder and sugar with milk and extract in small saucepan; stir over heat until mixture boils and thickens. Remove from heat; cover surface with plastic wrap, cool to room temperature.

{ **prep + cook time** 50 minutes (plus cooling time) **serves** 12 }

dutch ginger & almond slice

1¾ cups (260g) plain flour
1 cup (220g) caster sugar
⅔ cup (150g) coarsely chopped glacé ginger
½ cup (80g) blanched almonds, chopped coarsely
1 egg
185g butter, melted
2 teaspoons icing sugar

1 Preheat oven to 180°C/160°C fan-forced. Grease 20cm x 30cm lamington pan; line base and long sides with baking paper, extending paper 5cm above sides.
2 Combine sifted flour, sugar, ginger, nuts and egg in medium bowl; stir in butter.

3 Press mixture into pan; bake about 35 minutes. Stand slice in pan 10 minutes before lifting onto wire rack to cool. Dust with sifted icing sugar before cutting.

{**prep + cook time** 50 minutes **makes** 20}

raspberry coconut slice

90g butter, softened
½ cup (110g) caster sugar
1 egg
¼ cup (35g) self-raising flour
⅔ cup (100g) plain flour
1 tablespoon custard powder
⅔ cup (220g) raspberry jam
COCONUT TOPPING
2 cups (160g) desiccated coconut
¼ cup (55g) caster sugar
2 eggs, beaten lightly

1 Preheat oven to 180°C/160°C fan-forced. Grease 20cm x 30cm lamington pan; line base and long sides with baking paper, extending paper 5cm above sides.
2 Beat butter, sugar and egg in small bowl with electric mixer until light and fluffy. Transfer to medium bowl; stir in sifted flours and custard powder. Spread dough evenly into pan; spread with jam.

3 Make coconut topping; sprinkle topping over jam.
4 Bake about 40 minutes; cool slice in pan before cutting.
COCONUT TOPPING Combine ingredients in small bowl.

{ **prep + cook time** 1 hour **makes** 16 }

citrus poppy seed friands

6 egg whites
185g butter, melted
1 cup (120g) almond meal
1½ cups (240g) icing sugar
½ cup (75g) plain flour
1 tablespoon poppy seeds
2 teaspoons finely grated orange rind
1 teaspoon finely grated lemon rind

1 Preheat oven to 200°C/180°C fan-forced. Grease 12 x ½-cup (125ml) friand pans; place on oven tray.
2 Place egg whites in medium bowl; whisk lightly with fork until combined. Stir in remaining ingredients.

3 Divide mixture among pans; bake about 25 minutes. Stand friands in pans 5 minutes before turning, top-side up, onto wire rack to cool. Serve dusted with extra sifted icing sugar, if desired.

{ **prep + cook time** 45 minutes **makes** 12 }

berry muffins

2½ cups (375g) self-raising flour
90g cold butter, chopped
1 cup (220g) caster sugar
1¼ cups (310ml) buttermilk
1 egg, beaten lightly
200g fresh or frozen mixed berries

1 Preheat oven to 180°C/160°C fan-forced. Grease 12-hole (⅓-cup/80ml) muffin pan.
2 Sift flour into large bowl; rub in butter. Stir in sugar, buttermilk and egg. Do not overmix; mixture should be lumpy. Add berries; stir through gently.

3 Spoon mixture into pan holes; bake about 20 minutes. Stand muffins in pan 5 minutes before turning, top-side up, onto wire rack to cool.

{ **prep + cook time** 30 minutes **makes** 12 }

celebration fruit cake

3 cups (500g) sultanas
1¾ cups (300g) raisins, halved
1¾ cups (300g) dried dates, chopped finely
1 cup (150g) dried currants
⅔ cup (110g) mixed peel
⅔ cup (150g) glacé cherries, halved
¼ cup (50g) coarsely chopped glacé pineapple
¼ cup (60g) coarsely chopped glacé apricots
½ cup (125ml) dark rum
250g butter, softened
1 cup (220g) firmly packed brown sugar
5 eggs
1½ cups (225g) plain flour
⅓ cup (50g) self-raising flour
1 teaspoon mixed spice
2 tablespoons dark rum, extra

1 Combine fruit and rum in large bowl, mix well; cover tightly with plastic wrap. Store mixture in a cool, dark place overnight, or for up to a week, stirring every day.
2 Preheat oven to 150°C/130°C fan-forced. Line deep 22cm-round cake pan with three thicknesses of baking paper, extending paper 5cm above edge.

3 Beat butter and sugar in small bowl with electric mixer until just combined. Beat in eggs, one at a time.
4 Add butter mixture to fruit mixture; mix well. Mix in sifted dry ingredients; spread mixture evenly into prepared pan. Bake about 3½ hours.
5 Brush cake with extra rum. Cover hot cake tightly with foil; cool in pan.

{ **prep + cook time** 3 hours 50 minutes (plus standing & cooling time) **serves** 24 }

tip If cake starts to brown too much during baking, cover loosely with foil.

last-minute fruit cake

1½ cups (250g) sultanas
1 cup (150g) raisins, chopped coarsely
1 cup (150g) dried currants
½ cup (85g) mixed peel
⅓ cup (70g) glacé cherries, halved
2 tablespoons coarsely chopped glacé pineapple
2 tablespoons coarsely chopped glacé apricots
185g butter, chopped
¾ cup (165g) firmly packed brown sugar
⅓ cup (80ml) brandy
⅓ cup (80ml) water
2 teaspoons finely grated orange rind
1 teaspoon finely grated lemon rind
1 tablespoon treacle
3 eggs, beaten lightly
1¼ cups (185g) plain flour
¼ cup (35g) self-raising flour
½ teaspoon bicarbonate of soda
½ cup (80g) blanched almonds

1 Combine fruit, butter, sugar, brandy and the water in medium saucepan, stir over medium heat until butter is melted and sugar is dissolved; bring to the boil. Remove from heat; transfer to large bowl. Cool to room temperature.
2 Preheat oven to 150°C/130°C fan-forced. Line base and side of deep 20cm-round cake pan with three thicknesses of baking paper, extending paper 5cm above edge.
3 Stir rinds, treacle and egg into fruit mixture then stir in sifted dry ingredients. Spread mixture into pan; decorate with nuts. Bake about 2 hours.
4 Cover hot cake tightly with foil; cool in pan overnight.

{**prep + cook time** 2 hours 20 minutes (plus cooling time) **serves** 20}

rich sherried fruit cake

250g butter, softened
2 tablespoons plum jam
2 teaspoons finely grated orange rind
1¼ cups (275g) firmly packed brown sugar
5 eggs
¾ cup (180ml) sweet sherry
1½ cups (225g) plain flour
½ cup (75g) self-raising flour
2 teaspoons mixed spice
1kg (5 cups) mixed dried fruit
½ cup (125ml) sweet sherry, extra, warmed

1 Preheat oven to 150°C/130°C fan-forced. Line base and side of deep 22cm-round cake pan with four thicknesses of baking paper, extending paper 5cm above edge.
2 Beat butter, jam, rind and sugar in medium bowl with electric mixer until just combined. Beat in eggs, one at a time.
3 Stir in ½ cup of the sherry, sifted dry ingredients and fruit; mix well.

4 Spread mixture into pan. Bake about 3¼ hours.
5 Brush top of hot cake with remaining ¼ cup of sherry, cover hot cake with foil; cool in pan overnight.
6 Remove cake from pan, remove paper from cake. Brush cake all over with 2 tablespoons of the warmed extra sherry each week for 3 weeks.

{**prep + cook time** 3 hours 45 minutes (plus cooling and standing time) **serves** 20}

boiled pineapple rum cake

450g can crushed pineapple in syrup
1kg (5 cups) mixed dried fruit
250g butter, chopped coarsely
1 cup (220g) firmly packed brown sugar
2 tablespoons orange marmalade
2 tablespoons dark rum
4 eggs, beaten lightly
1⅔ cups (250g) plain flour
⅓ cup (50g) self-raising flour
½ teaspoon bicarbonate of soda
1 tablespoon dark rum, extra

1 Drain pineapple over large jug; discard ½ cup of the syrup.
2 Combine pineapple, remaining syrup, fruit, butter, sugar, marmalade and rum in large saucepan. Using wooden spoon, stir over heat until butter melts and sugar dissolves; bring to the boil. Reduce heat; simmer, covered, 10 minutes. Cool to room temperature.

3 Preheat oven to 150°C/130°C fan-forced. Line base and side of deep 20cm-round cake pan with three thicknesses baking paper, extending paper 5cm above edges.
4 Using wooden spoon, stir egg and sifted dry ingredients into fruit mixture. Pour mixture into pan; bake about 2 hours.
5 Brush hot cake with extra rum. Cover pan tightly with foil; cool cake in pan.

{**prep + cook time** 2 hours 20 minutes (plus cooling time) **serves** 20}

rock cakes

2 cups (300g) self-raising flour
¼ teaspoon ground cinnamon
⅓ cup (75g) caster sugar
90g cold butter, chopped
1 cup (160g) sultanas
1 egg, beaten lightly
½ cup (125ml) milk
1 tablespoon caster sugar, extra

1 Preheat oven to 200°C/180°C fan-forced. Grease oven trays.
2 Sift flour, cinnamon and sugar into medium bowl; rub in butter. Stir in sultanas, egg and milk. Do not overmix.

3 Drop rounded tablespoons of mixture about 5cm apart onto trays; sprinkle with extra sugar. Bake about 15 minutes; cool cakes on trays.

{ **prep + cook time** 30 minutes **makes** 18 }

carrot cake with lemon cream cheese frosting

You need three large carrots (540g) for this recipe.

1 cup (250ml) vegetable oil
1⅓ cups (295g) firmly packed brown sugar
3 eggs
3 cups firmly packed, coarsely grated carrot
1 cup (110g) coarsely chopped walnuts
2½ cups (375g) self-raising flour
½ teaspoon bicarbonate of soda
2 teaspoons mixed spice
LEMON CREAM CHEESE FROSTING
30g butter, softened
80g cream cheese, softened
1 teaspoon finely grated lemon rind
1½ cups (240g) icing sugar

1 Preheat oven to 180°C/160°C fan-forced. Grease deep 22cm-round cake pan; line base with baking paper.
2 Beat oil, sugar and eggs in small bowl with electric mixer until thick and creamy. Transfer mixture to large bowl; stir in carrot, nuts then sifted dry ingredients.
3 Pour mixture into pan; bake about 1¼ hours. Stand cake in pan 5 minutes before turning, top-side up, onto wire rack to cool.
4 Meanwhile, make lemon cream cheese frosting. Spread cake with frosting.
LEMON CREAM CHEESE FROSTING Beat butter, cream cheese and rind in small bowl with electric mixer until light and fluffy; gradually beat in sifted icing sugar.

{**prep + cook time** 1 hour 45 minutes **serves** 12}

upside-down toffee banana cake

You need four bananas for this recipe; two large overripe bananas weighing about 460g to make 1 cup of mashed banana, and two medium bananas.

1 cup (220g) caster sugar
1 cup (250ml) water
2 medium bananas (400g), sliced thinly
2 eggs, beaten lightly
⅔ cup (160ml) vegetable oil
¾ cup (165g) firmly packed brown sugar
1 teaspoon vanilla extract
⅔ cup (100g) plain flour
⅓ cup (50g) wholemeal self-raising flour
2 teaspoons mixed spice
1 teaspoon bicarbonate of soda
1 cup mashed banana

1 Preheat oven to 180°C/160°C fan-forced. Grease deep 22cm-round cake pan; line base with baking paper.
2 Stir caster sugar and the water in medium saucepan over heat, without boiling, until sugar dissolves; bring to the boil. Boil, uncovered, without stirring, about 10 minutes or until caramel in colour. Pour toffee into prepared pan; top with sliced banana.

3 Combine egg, oil, brown sugar and extract in medium bowl. Stir in sifted dry ingredients, then mashed banana.
4 Pour mixture into pan; bake about 40 minutes. Turn cake onto serving plate; peel off baking paper. Serve cake, warm or at room temperature, with thick cream, if desired.

{**prep + cook time** 1 hour 10 minutes **serves** 10}

dundee cake

180g butter, softened
¾ cup (165g) caster sugar
5 eggs, lightly beaten
1½ cups (225g) plain flour
½ cup (75g) self-raising flour
½ teaspoon mixed spice
⅓ cup (80ml) milk
1¼ cups (200g) raisins, chopped coarsely
1½ cups (250g) currants
1¼ cups (200g) sultanas
⅓ cup (70g) red glacé cherries, chopped coarsely
2 tablespoons mixed peel
½ cup (80g) blanched almonds
1 tablespoon brandy

1 Preheat oven to 150°C/130°C fan-forced. Line deep 19cm-square cake pan with three layers of baking paper, extending paper 5cm above edges.
2 Beat butter, sugar, egg, sifted dry ingredients and milk in large bowl with electric mixer on medium speed about 3 minutes or until mixture becomes pale in colour. Stir in fruit and half the nuts.
3 Spread mixture into pan; decorate top with remaining nuts. Bake about 2 hours. Brush hot cake with brandy; cover tightly with foil, cool in pan.

{ **prep + cook time** 3 hours 20 minutes (plus cooling time) **serves** 16 }

siena cake

¾ cup (120g) blanched almonds, roasted, chopped coarsely
1 cup (140g) coarsely chopped roasted hazelnuts
¼ cup (80g) finely chopped glacé apricots
¼ cup (55g) finely chopped glacé pineapple
⅓ cup (55g) mixed peel, chopped finely
⅔ cup (100g) plain flour
2 tablespoons cocoa powder
1 teaspoon ground cinnamon
⅓ cup (75g) caster sugar
½ cup (180g) honey
60g dark eating chocolate, melted

1 Preheat oven to 170°C/150°C fan-forced. Grease deep 20cm-round cake pan; line base and side with baking paper.
2 Combine nuts, apricots, pineapple, mixed peel, and sifted flour, cocoa and cinnamon in large bowl; mix well.
3 Place sugar and honey in medium saucepan; stir over low heat until sugar dissolves, brushing down side of pan to dissolve any sugar crystals. Bring to the boil; reduce heat, simmer, uncovered, about 5 minutes or until syrup forms a soft ball when a few drops of the syrup are dropped into a glass of cold water.
4 Add syrup and chocolate to fruit and nut mixture; mix well. Spread mixture quickly into pan; bake about 35 minutes. Cool cake in pan. Turn out cake; remove paper. Wrap cake in foil; stand overnight.

{ **prep + cook time** 1 hour 30 minutes (plus cooling and standing time) **serves** 8 }

zucchini walnut loaf

You need 3 medium zucchinis (360g), for this recipe.

3 eggs
1½ cups (330g) firmly packed brown sugar
1 cup (250ml) vegetable oil
1½ cups finely grated zucchini
1 cup (110g) coarsely chopped walnuts
1½ cups (225g) self-raising flour
1½ cups (225g) plain flour

1 Preheat oven to 180°C/160°C fan-forced. Grease 15cm x 25cm loaf pan; line base and long sides with baking paper, extending paper 5cm above edges.
2 Beat eggs, sugar and oil in large bowl with electric mixer until combined. Stir in zucchini, walnuts and sifted flours in two batches.
3 Spread mixture into pan; bake about 1¼ hours. Stand cake in pan 5 minutes before turning, top-side up, onto wire rack to cool. Serve with butter if you like.

{ **prep + cook time** 1 hour 30 minutes **serves** 10 }

CLASSIC

Syrup cakes

4

Syrup-soaked cakes are at their best
served warm, either just as they are with
a good cup of tea or coffee, or as a dessert
with a dollop of cream and maybe some
fresh fruit that ties in with the flavour of
the cake. Slices of cake can be reheated
gently in a microwave oven.

mixed berry cake with vanilla bean syrup

125g butter, softened
1 cup (220g) caster sugar
3 eggs
½ cup (75g) plain flour
¼ cup (35g) self-raising flour
½ cup (60g) almond meal
⅓ cup (80g) sour cream
1½ cups (225g) frozen mixed berries
½ cup (100g) drained canned seeded black cherries
VANILLA BEAN SYRUP
½ cup (125ml) water
½ cup (110g) caster sugar
2 vanilla beans

1 Preheat oven to 180°C/160°C fan-forced. Grease 21cm baba pan thoroughly (or grease deep 20cm-round cake pan and line base and side with baking paper).
2 Beat butter and sugar in small bowl with electric mixer until light and fluffy. Beat in eggs, one at a time. Transfer mixture to large bowl; stir in sifted flours, almond meal, sour cream, berries and cherries. Pour mixture into pan; bake about 40 minutes.
3 Meanwhile, make vanilla bean syrup.

4 Stand cake in pan 5 minutes before turning onto wire rack set over tray. Pour hot syrup over hot cake.
VANILLA BEAN SYRUP Combine the water and sugar in small saucepan. Split vanilla beans in half lengthways; scrape seeds into pan then place pods in pan. Stir over heat, without boiling, until sugar dissolves. Simmer, uncovered, without stirring, 5 minutes. Using tongs, remove pods from syrup.

{ **prep + cook time** 1 hour **serves** 8 }

orange poppy seed syrup cake

⅓ cup (50g) poppy seeds
¼ cup (60ml) milk
185g butter, softened
1 tablespoon finely grated orange rind
1 cup (220g) caster sugar
3 eggs
1½ cups (225g) self-raising flour
½ cup (75g) plain flour
½ cup (60g) almond meal
½ cup (125ml) orange juice
ORANGE SYRUP
1 cup (220g) caster sugar
⅔ cup (160ml) orange juice
⅓ cup (80ml) water

1 Combine seeds and milk in small bowl; stand 20 minutes.
2 Preheat oven to 180°C/160°C fan-forced. Grease deep 22cm-round cake pan; line base and side with baking paper.
3 Beat butter, rind and sugar in small bowl with electric mixer until light and fluffy; beat in eggs, one at a time. Transfer mixture to large bowl; using wooden spoon, stir in flours, almond meal, juice and poppy-seed mixture. Spread mixture into pan; bake about 1 hour.

4 Meanwhile, make orange syrup.
5 Stand cake in pan 5 minutes before turning, top-side up, onto wire rack set over tray. Pour hot syrup over hot cake; serve warm.
ORANGE SYRUP Using wooden spoon, stir ingredients in small saucepan over heat, without boiling, until sugar dissolves. Bring to the boil; reduce heat, simmer, uncovered, without stirring, 2 minutes.

{**prep + cook time** 1 hour 25 minutes (plus standing time) **serves** 16}

lemon syrup cake

250g butter, softened
1 tablespoon finely grated lemon rind
1 cup (220g) caster sugar
3 eggs
1 cup (250ml) buttermilk
⅓ cup (80ml) lemon juice
2 cups (300g) self-raising flour
LEMON SYRUP
⅓ cup (80ml) lemon juice
¼ cup (60ml) water
¾ cup (165g) caster sugar

1 Preheat oven to 180°C/160°C fan-forced. Grease 24cm baba pan (or grease deep 22cm-round cake pan and line base and side with baking paper).
2 Beat butter, rind and sugar in small bowl with electric mixer until light and fluffy. Beat in eggs, one at a time. Transfer mixture to large bowl; fold in buttermilk, juice and sifted flour, in two batches.
3 Spread mixture into pan; bake about 50 minutes if using baba pan or bake about 1 hour if using round pan. Cover cake with foil if browning too quickly.
4 Meanwhile, make lemon syrup.
5 Stand cake in pan 5 minutes before turning onto wire rack set over tray. Pour hot syrup over hot cake; serve warm.
LEMON SYRUP Combine ingredients in small saucepan; stir over heat, without boiling, until sugar dissolves. Simmer, uncovered, without stirring, 5 minutes.

{**prep + cook time** 1 hour 10 minutes **serves** 12}

orange syrup cake

1 large orange (300g)
2 cups (500ml) water
2 cups (440g) caster sugar
⅔ cup (160ml) brandy
250g unsalted butter, softened
1 cup (220g) caster sugar, extra
4 eggs
1½ cups (225g) self-raising flour
2 tablespoons cornflour

1 Preheat oven to 160°C/140°C fan-forced. Grease deep 22cm-round cake pan; line base and side with baking paper.
2 Peel orange. Chop peel and flesh of orange finely; discard seeds. Stir flesh and peel in medium saucepan with the water, sugar and brandy, over medium heat, until sugar dissolves; bring to the boil. Reduce heat; simmer, uncovered, about 15 minutes or until orange skin is tender. Strain syrup into heatproof jug; reserve orange solids separately.
3 Beat butter and extra sugar in small bowl with electric mixer until light and fluffy. Beat in eggs, one at a time. Transfer mixture to large bowl. Stir in combined sifted flours, and reserved orange solids. Pour mixture into pan; bake about 50 minutes.
4 Meanwhile, simmer reserved syrup over heat in small saucepan until thickened slightly.
5 Stand cake in pan 5 minutes before turning, top-side up, onto wire rack set over tray. Pour hot syrup over hot cake; serve warm.

{ **prep + cook time** 1 hour 35 minutes **serves** 12 }

banana butterscotch syrup cake

You will need 2 large overripe bananas (460g) for this recipe.

125g butter, softened
¾ cup (165g) caster sugar
2 eggs
1 cup mashed banana
¾ cup (110g) self-raising flour
¾ cup (110g) plain flour
½ teaspoon bicarbonate of soda
¾ cup (110g) hazelnuts, roasted, chopped finely
BUTTERSCOTCH SYRUP
½ cup (110g) firmly packed brown sugar
30g butter, chopped
¾ cup (180ml) water

1 Preheat oven to 180°C/160°C fan-forced. Grease deep 19cm-square cake pan; line base with baking paper.
2 Beat butter and sugar in medium bowl with electric mixer until light and fluffy. Beat in eggs, one at a time. Stir in banana, then combined sifted flours and soda, and nuts. Spread mixture into pan; bake about 1 hour.

3 Meanwhile, make butterscotch syrup.
4 Stand cake in pan 5 minutes before turning, top-side up, onto wire rack set over tray. Drizzle hot syrup over hot cake.
BUTTERSCOTCH SYRUP Combine sugar and butter in small saucepan; stir over heat until butter melts. Add the water and bring to the boil, stirring; remove from heat.

{ **prep + cook time** 1 hour 15 minutes **serves** 9 }

semolina and yogurt lemon-syrup cake

250g butter, softened
1 tablespoon finely grated lemon rind
1 cup (220g) caster sugar
3 eggs, separated
1 cup (150g) self-raising flour
1 cup (180g) semolina
1 cup (280g) yogurt
LEMON SYRUP
1 cup (220g) caster sugar
1/3 cup (80ml) lemon juice

1 Preheat oven to 180°C/160°C fan-forced. Grease 20cm baba pan (or grease deep 20cm-round cake pan and line base and side with baking paper).
2 Beat butter, rind and sugar in small bowl with electric mixer until light and fluffy. Beat in egg yolks. Transfer mixture to large bowl; stir in sifted flour, semolina and yogurt.
3 Beat egg whites in small bowl with electric mixer until soft peaks form; fold egg whites into cake mixture, in two batches. Spread mixture into pan; bake about 50 minutes.
4 Meanwhile, make lemon syrup.
5 Stand cake in pan 5 minutes before turning onto wire rack set over tray. Pierce cake all over with skewer; pour hot lemon syrup over hot cake.
LEMON SYRUP Combine ingredients in small saucepan; stir over heat, without boiling, until sugar dissolves. Bring to the boil, without stirring, then remove from heat.

{ **prep + cook time** 1 hour 10 minutes **serves** 8 }

espresso syrup cake

3 teaspoons instant espresso coffee granules
1 tablespoon hot water
3 eggs
¾ cup (165g) caster sugar
1 cup (150g) self-raising flour
1 tablespoon cocoa powder
150g butter, melted
ESPRESSO SYRUP
¾ cup (165g) caster sugar
¾ cup (180ml) water
3 teaspoons instant espresso coffee granules

1 Preheat oven to 180°C/160°C fan-forced. Grease 20cm baba pan (or grease deep 20cm-round cake pan and line base and side with baking paper).
2 Combine coffee and the water in small jug; stir until dissolved.
3 Beat eggs in small bowl with electric mixer about 8 minutes or until thick and creamy; gradually add sugar, beating until dissolved between additions. Fold in sifted flour and cocoa, then butter and coffee mixture. Pour mixture into pan; bake about 40 minutes.

4 Meanwhile, make espresso syrup.
5 Stand cake in pan 5 minutes before turning onto wire rack set over tray. Reserve ¼ cup espresso syrup; drizzle remaining hot syrup over hot cake. Serve with reserved syrup.
ESPRESSO SYRUP Combine ingredients in small saucepan; stir over heat, without boiling, until sugar dissolves. Bring to the boil then remove from heat.

{ **prep + cook time** 1 hour **serves** 8 }

cinnamon and walnut syrup cake

3 eggs
¾ cup (165g) caster sugar
¾ cup (110g) self-raising flour
3 teaspoons ground cinnamon
185g butter, melted
¾ cup (80g) coarsely chopped walnuts
SUGAR SYRUP
1 cup (220) caster sugar
¾ cup (180ml) water

1 Preheat oven to 180°C/160°C fan-forced. Grease 23cm-square slab pan; line base with baking paper.
2 Beat eggs in small bowl with electric mixer until thick and creamy. Gradually add sugar, beating until dissolved between additions. Beat in sifted flour and cinnamon, in two batches; beat in butter then stir in nuts. Pour mixture into pan; bake about 30 minutes.

3 Meanwhile, make sugar syrup.
4 Stand cake in pan 5 minutes before turning onto wire rack set over tray. Pour hot syrup over hot cake. Serve cake warm or cold.
SUGAR SYRUP Combine ingredients in small saucepan; stir constantly over heat without boiling until sugar is dissolved. Bring to the boil; reduce heat, simmer, uncovered, 5 minutes.

{**prep + cook time** 1 hour **serves** 12}

lime syrup buttermilk cake

250g butter, softened
1 tablespoon finely grated lime rind
1 cup (220g) caster sugar
3 eggs, separated
2 cups (300g) self-raising flour
1 cup (250ml) buttermilk
LIME SYRUP
⅓ cup (80ml) lime juice
¾ cup (165g) caster sugar
¼ cup (60ml) water

1 Preheat oven to 180°C/160°C fan-forced. Grease 20cm baba pan (or grease deep 20cm-round cake pan and line base and side with baking paper).
2 Beat butter, rind and sugar in small bowl with electric mixer until light and fluffy; beat in egg yolks, one at a time, until combined. Transfer mixture to large bowl; stir in sifted flour, and buttermilk, in two batches.
3 Beat egg whites in small bowl with electric mixer until soft peaks form; fold into flour mixture, in two batches. Spread mixture into pan; bake about 1 hour.
4 Meanwhile, make lime syrup.
5 Stand cake in pan 5 minutes before turning onto serving plate. Gradually pour hot lime syrup evenly over hot cake. Serve cake sprinkled with thinly sliced lime rind, if desired.
LIME SYRUP Combine ingredients in small saucepan; stir over heat, without boiling, until sugar is dissolved. Bring to the boil; remove from heat.

{ **prep + cook time** 1 hour 30 minutes **serves** 8 }

glacé fruit cake

185g butter, softened
½ cup (110g) caster sugar
3 eggs
1 cup (250g) finely chopped glacé apricot
½ cup (80g) finely chopped glacé orange
½ cup (90g) finely chopped glacé ginger
¾ cup (210g) finely chopped glacé fig
1½ cups (225g) plain flour
½ cup (75g) self-raising flour
½ cup (125ml) milk
¼ cup (60ml) ginger wine
GINGER SYRUP
¼ cup (60ml) ginger wine
¼ cup (60ml) water
¼ cup (55g) caster sugar
2 teaspoons lemon juice

1 Preheat oven to 150°C/130°C fan-forced. Line base and long sides of 14cm x 21cm loaf pan with baking paper, extending paper 5cm above sides.
2 Beat butter and sugar in small bowl with electric mixer until just combined. Beat in eggs, one at a time. Transfer mixture to large bowl; stir in fruit then combined sifted flours, and combined milk and wine, in two batches. Spread mixture into pan; bake about 2½ hours.

3 Meanwhile, make ginger syrup.
4 Pour hot ginger syrup over hot cake in pan. Cover cake with foil; cool in pan.
GINGER SYRUP Stir ingredients in small saucepan over low heat, without boiling, until sugar dissolves; bring to the boil. Boil, uncovered, without stirring, about 2 minutes or until syrup thickens slightly.

{ **prep + cook time** 2 hours 50 minutes (plus cooling time) **serves** 12 }

tip Ginger wine, a beverage that is 14% alcohol by volume, has the piquant taste of fresh ginger. You can substitute it with dry (white) vermouth, if you prefer.

almond orange halva cake

125g butter, softened
2 teaspoons finely grated orange rind
½ cup (110g) caster sugar
2 eggs
1 teaspoon baking powder
1 cup (180g) semolina
1 cup (120g) almond meal
¼ cup (60ml) orange juice
ORANGE AND BRANDY SYRUP
1 cup (250ml) orange juice
½ cup (110g) caster sugar
1 tablespoon brandy

1 Preheat oven to 180°C/160°C fan-forced. Grease deep 20cm-round cake pan; line base and side with baking paper.
2 Cream butter, rind and sugar in small bowl with electric mixer until light and fluffy. Beat in eggs, one at a time, until combined. Transfer mixture to large bowl; stir in dry ingredients and juice in two batches. Spread mixture into pan; bake about 40 minutes.
3 Meanwhile, make orange and brandy syrup.

4 Turn cake, top-side up, onto wire rack set over oven tray; brush half the hot syrup over hot cake. Bake (on wire rack) a further 5 minutes. Remove from oven; brush with remaining hot syrup. Serve cake warm or cold.
ORANGE AND BRANDY SYRUP Combine juice and sugar in small saucepan; stir constantly over heat, without boiling, until sugar is dissolved. Bring to the boil; reduce heat, simmer, uncovered, without stirring, 5 minutes. Stir in brandy.

{ **prep + cook time** 1 hour 15 minutes **serves** 10 }

CLASSIC

Dessert cakes

5

Forget the diet, think luscious indulgence.
Most dessert cakes take a little time
and effort to make, but usually they
can be made at least a day ahead of
serving. Leave any assembling, filling
and decorating until the last minute
for maximum effect.

black forest cake

250g butter, chopped
1 tablespoon instant coffee granules
1½ cups (375ml) hot water
200g dark eating chocolate, chopped
2 cups (440g) caster sugar
1½ cups (225g) self-raising flour
1 cup (150g) plain flour
¼ cup (25g) cocoa powder
2 eggs
2 teaspoons vanilla extract
¼ cup (60ml) kirsch
600ml thickened cream, whipped
2 x 425g cans seeded black cherries, drained, halved
2 teaspoons cocoa powder, extra

1 Preheat oven to 150°C/130°C fan-forced. Grease deep 22cm-round cake pan, line base and side with baking paper.
2 Melt butter in medium saucepan; stir in combined coffee and hot water, then chocolate and sugar. Stir over low heat, without boiling, until smooth. Transfer mixture to large bowl, cool to warm.
3 Beat chocolate mixture on low speed with electric mixer; gradually beat in sifted dry ingredients, in three batches. Beat in eggs, one at a time, then extract.

4 Pour mixture into pan; bake about 1¾ hours. Stand cake in pan 5 minutes before turning, top-side up, onto wire rack to cool.
5 Trim top of cake to make it flat. Split cake into three even layers. Place one layer onto serving plate; brush with half of the kirsch, top with half of the cream and half of the cherries. Repeat layering, then top with cake top. Dust with extra sifted cocoa.

{ **prep + cook time** 2 hours 25 minutes (plus cooling time) **serves** 12 }

warm apple cake with brandy butterscotch sauce

125g butter, softened
½ cup (110g) caster sugar
2 eggs
⅔ cup (100g) self-raising flour
⅓ cup (50g) plain flour
1 tablespoon milk
3 medium green-skinned apples (450g)
½ cup (160g) apricot jam, warmed
BRANDY BUTTERSCOTCH SAUCE
½ cup (100g) firmly packed brown sugar
½ cup (125ml) thickened cream
100g butter, chopped
2 tablespoons brandy

1 Preheat oven to 160°C/140°C fan-forced. Grease two 8cm x 25cm bar cake pans; line bases and long sides with baking paper, extending paper 5cm above sides.
2 Beat butter and sugar in small bowl with electric mixer until light and fluffy. Beat in eggs, one at a time. Stir in sifted flours and milk; spread mixture into pans.
3 Peel, core and halve apples; slice each half thinly. Push apple slices gently into surface of cake mixture. Brush apple with jam; bake about 40 minutes.

4 Make brandy butterscotch sauce.
5 Stand cakes in pans 10 minutes before turning, top-sides up, onto wire racks to cool. Serve pieces of warm cake drizzled with brandy butterscotch sauce.
BRANDY BUTTERSCOTCH SAUCE
Combine ingredients in small saucepan. Stir over heat, without boiling, until sugar dissolves; bring to the boil. Reduce heat; simmer, uncovered, without stirring, about 3 minutes or until mixture thickens slightly.

{ **prep + cook time** 1 hour 10 minutes **serves** 8 }

chocolate roulade with coffee cream

200g dark eating chocolate, chopped coarsely
¼ cup (60ml) hot water
1 tablespoon instant coffee granules
4 eggs, separated
½ cup (110g) caster sugar
1 tablespoon caster sugar, extra
1 teaspoon hot water, extra
300ml thickened cream
2 tablespoons coffee-flavoured liqueur
1 tablespoon icing sugar

1 Preheat oven to 180°C/160°C fan-forced. Grease 25cm x 30cm swiss roll pan; line base and long sides with baking paper, extending paper 5cm above sides.
2 Combine chocolate, the water and half the coffee granules in large heatproof bowl. Stir mixture over large saucepan of simmering water until smooth (do not allow water to touch base of bowl); remove from heat.
3 Beat egg yolks and caster sugar in small bowl with electric mixer until thick and creamy; fold egg mixture into warm chocolate mixture.
4 Beat egg whites in small bowl with electric mixer until soft peaks form; fold egg whites into chocolate mixture, in two batches. Spread into pan; bake about 10 minutes.
5 Meanwhile, place piece of baking paper cut the same size as pan on bench; sprinkle with extra caster sugar. Turn hot cake onto paper; peel lining paper away. Cool, then trim sides of cake. Cover cake with tea-towel.
6 Dissolve remaining coffee granules in the extra water in small bowl. Add cream, liqueur and sifted icing sugar; beat with electric mixer until firm peaks form. Spread cake evenly with cream mixture. Using paper as a guide, roll cake from long side. Cover roll; refrigerate 30 minutes before serving.

{ **prep + cook time** 30 minutes (plus cooling & refrigeration time) **serves** 8 }

vanilla pear almond cake

8 corella pears (800g)
2½ cups (625ml) water
1 strip lemon rind
1¾ cups (385g) caster sugar
1 vanilla bean, halved lengthways
125g butter, softened
3 eggs
⅔ cup (160g) sour cream
⅔ cup (100g) plain flour
⅔ cup (100g) self-raising flour
¼ cup (40g) blanched almonds, roasted, chopped coarsely
40g dark eating chocolate, chopped
½ cup (60g) almond meal

1 Peel pears, leaving stems intact.
2 Combine the water, rind and 1 cup of the sugar in medium saucepan. Scrape vanilla bean seeds into saucepan, then place pod in saucepan. Stir over heat, without boiling, until sugar dissolves. Add pears; bring to the boil. Reduce heat; simmer, covered, about 30 minutes or until pears are just tender. Transfer pears to medium bowl; bring syrup to the boil. Boil, uncovered, until syrup reduces by half. Using tongs, remove vanilla pod. Cool syrup completely.
3 Preheat oven to 200°C/180°C fan-forced. Insert base of 23cm springform tin upside down in tin to give a flat base; grease tin.
4 Beat butter and remaining sugar in medium bowl with electric mixer until light and fluffy. Beat in eggs, one at a time. Add sour cream; beat until just combined. Stir in 2 tablespoons of the syrup, then combined sifted flours, nuts, chocolate and almond meal.
5 Spread mixture into tin; place pears upright around edge of tin, gently pushing pears to the bottom. Bake about 1 hour 35 minutes. Stand cake 10 minutes before removing from tin.
6 Serve cake warm, brushed with remaining syrup.

{ **prep + cook time** 2 hours 45 minutes (plus cooling time) **serves** 8 }

soft-centred mocha puddings

150g dark chocolate, chopped
125g butter, chopped
3 teaspoons instant coffee granules
2 eggs
2 egg yolks
⅓ cup (75g) caster sugar
¼ cup (35g) plain flour
2 teaspoons cocoa powder

1 Preheat oven to 200°C/180°C fan-forced. Grease six-hole (¾-cup/180ml) texas muffin pan well with softened butter.
2 Stir chocolate, butter and coffee in small saucepan, over low heat, until smooth; cool 10 minutes. Transfer mixture to a large bowl.
3 Beat eggs, egg yolks and sugar in small bowl with electric mixer until thick and creamy. Fold egg mixture and sifted flour into barely warm chocolate mixture.
4 Divide mixture among pan holes; bake, in oven, 12 minutes.
5 Gently turn puddings, top-side down, onto serving plates. Serve immediately, dusted with sifted cocoa powder.

{ **prep + cook time** 40 minutes **makes** 6 }

tip Use a good-quality dark chocolate with 70% cocoa solids.

flourless chocolate dessert cake

100g dark eating chocolate, chopped
100g butter, chopped
½ cup (110g) caster sugar
2 tablespoons marsala
⅔ cup (80g) almond meal
1 tablespoon instant coffee granules
1 tablespoon hot water
3 eggs, separated
STRAWBERRY COULIS
250g strawberries
¼ cup (40g) icing sugar

1 Preheat oven to 180°C/160°C fan-forced. Grease deep 20cm-round cake pan; line base and side with baking paper.
2 Melt chocolate and butter in small saucepan, over low heat, stirring, until mixture is combined.
3 Combine chocolate mixture with sugar, marsala, almond meal and combined coffee and the water in a large bowl; beat in egg yolks, one at a time.
4 Beat egg whites in small bowl with electric mixer until soft peaks form; gently fold into chocolate mixture, in two batches.

5 Pour mixture into pan; bake about 45 minutes. Cool cake in pan, cover; refrigerate several hours or overnight.
6 Make strawberry coulis.
7 Carefully turn cake onto board; cut into slices with a hot knife. Serve cake with strawberry coulis. Dust with sifted icing sugar and serve with whipped cream, if you like.
STRAWBERRY COULIS Blend or process ingredients until mixture is smooth.

{ **prep + cook time** 1 hour (plus refrigeration time) **serves** 6 }

rich truffle mud cake

6 eggs
½ cup (110g) firmly packed brown sugar
400g dark eating chocolate, melted
1 cup (250ml) thick cream (48% fat content)
⅓ cup (80ml) Cointreau

1 Preheat oven to 180°C/160°C fan-forced. Grease deep 22cm-round cake pan; line base and side with baking paper.
2 Beat eggs and sugar in large bowl with electric mixer until thick and creamy. With motor operating, gradually beat in barely warm melted chocolate until combined. Using metal spoon, gently fold in combined cream and liqueur.
3 Pour mixture into pan. Place pan in baking dish; pour enough boiling water into dish to come halfway up side of pan. Bake about 30 minutes. Cover pan loosely with foil; bake about 30 minutes. Discard foil; remove pan from dish, cool cake in pan.
4 Turn cake onto serving plate, cover; refrigerate overnight. Serve dusted with a little sifted cocoa, if desired. Goes well served with a raspberry coulis and fresh raspberries.

{**prep + cook time** 1 hour 15 minutes (plus cooling and refrigeration time) **serves** 12}

dark chocolate & almond torte

160g dark eating chocolate, chopped
160g unsalted butter, chopped
5 eggs, separated
¾ cup (165g) caster sugar
1 cup (120g) almond meal
⅔ cup (50g) flaked almonds, roasted, chopped coarsely
⅓ cup (35g) coarsely grated dark eating chocolate
1 cup (150g) vienna almonds
DARK CHOCOLATE GANACHE
125g dark eating chocolate, chopped
⅓ cup (80ml) thickened cream

1 Preheat oven to 180°C/160°C fan-forced. Grease deep 22cm-round cake pan; line the base and side with two layers of baking paper.
2 Stir chopped chocolate and butter in small saucepan over low heat until smooth; cool to room temperature.
3 Beat egg yolks and sugar in small bowl with electric mixer until thick and creamy. Transfer mixture to large bowl; fold in chocolate mixture, almond meal, flaked almonds and grated chocolate.
4 Beat egg whites in small bowl with electric mixer until soft peaks form; fold into chocolate mixture, in two batches.
5 Pour mixture into pan; bake about 45 minutes. Stand cake in pan 15 minutes before turning, top-side up, onto wire rack to cool.
6 Make dark chocolate ganache.
7 Spread ganache over cake, decorate with vienna almonds; stand 30 minutes before serving.
DARK CHOCOLATE GANACHE Stir ingredients in small saucepan over low heat until smooth.

{**prep + cook time** 1 hour 15 minutes (plus cooling & standing time) **serves** 14}

opera gateau

4 eggs
1¼ cups (150g) almond meal
1 cup (160g) icing sugar
⅓ cup (50g) plain flour
25g unsalted butter, melted
4 egg whites
1 tablespoon caster sugar
COFFEE BUTTER CREAM
¼ cup (60ml) milk
¼ cup (55g) brown sugar
2 teaspoons instant coffee granules
1 egg yolk
125g unsalted butter, softened

COFFEE SYRUP
⅓ cup (80ml) boiling water
2 tablespoons caster sugar
1 tablespoon instant coffee granules
GANACHE
160g dark eating chocolate,
chopped coarsely
⅓ cup (80ml) cream
GLAZE
50g unsalted butter, chopped
75g dark eating chocolate

1 Preheat oven to 220°C/200°C fan-forced. Grease two 25cm x 30cm swiss roll pans; line bases with baking paper, extending paper 5cm over long sides.
2 Beat eggs, meal and sifted icing sugar in small bowl with electric mixer until creamy; beat in flour. Transfer mixture to large bowl; stir in butter. Beat egg whites in small bowl with electric mixer until soft peaks form; add caster sugar, beating until sugar dissolves. Fold into almond mixture, in two batches. Divide mixture between pans. Bake 7 minutes. Cool.
3 Make coffee butter cream, coffee syrup, and ganache.
4 Cut each cake into a 20cm x 25cm rectangle and a 10cm x 25cm rectangle. Place one of the large cake rectangles on baking-paper-lined tray; brush with half the coffee syrup then spread cake with half the butter cream. Refrigerate 10 minutes. Top butter cream with the two small cake rectangles, side-by-side. Brush tops with the remaining coffee syrup then spread with ganache. Top with remaining cake; refrigerate 10 minutes. Spread remaining butter cream over top of cake; refrigerate 3 hours. Make glaze.
5 Quickly spread glaze evenly over cake. Refrigerate 30 minutes or until set.
COFFEE BUTTER CREAM Stir milk, sugar and coffee in small saucepan, over low heat, until sugar dissolves. Whisk yolk in small bowl; gradually whisk in hot milk mixture. Return custard to pan; stir over heat, without boiling, about 5 minutes or until thickened slightly. Cool. Beat butter in small bowl with electric mixer until light and fluffy; beat in custard.
COFFEE SYRUP Combine ingredients in small bowl.
GANACHE Stir ingredients in small heatproof bowl over small saucepan of simmering water until smooth. Refrigerate until spreadable.
GLAZE Stir ingredients in small heatproof bowl over small saucepan of simmering water until smooth. Use while warm.

{ **prep + cook time** 1 hour (plus cooling and refrigeration time) **serves** 24 }

rum baba

7g sachet dry yeast
¼ cup (35g) plain flour
¼ cup (60ml) warm milk
¾ cup (110g) plain flour, extra
2 tablespoons caster sugar
2 eggs, beaten lightly
60g butter, melted
RUM SYRUP
1½ cups (330g) caster sugar
1 cup (250ml) water
2 tablespoons dark rum

1 Grease six ½-cup (125ml) moulds.
2 Mix yeast with flour and milk in small bowl; cover, stand in warm place about 10 minutes or until mixture is frothy.
3 Sift extra flour and sugar into large bowl; stir in yeast mixture, egg and butter. Beat about 3 minutes with a wooden spoon until batter is smooth. Place batter in large greased bowl, cover; stand in warm place about 40 minutes or until batter has doubled in size.
4 Preheat oven to 200°C/180°C fan-forced.
5 Beat batter again. Divide batter between moulds; stand, uncovered, until batter rises three-quarters of the way up side of moulds. Place moulds on oven tray; bake about 15 minutes.
6 Meanwhile, make rum syrup.
7 Turn babas onto wire rack set over tray; pour hot rum syrup over hot babas. Place babas on serving plates; pour syrup from tray over babas until all syrup has been absorbed.
RUM SYRUP Combine sugar and the water in small saucepan; stir over heat, without boiling, until sugar is dissolved. Bring to the boil; boil, uncovered, without stirring, 2 minutes. Remove from heat, stir in rum.

{**prep + cook time** 40 minutes (plus standing time) **makes** 6}

italian ricotta cheesecake

90g butter, softened
¼ cup (55g) caster sugar
1 egg
1¼ cups (185g) plain flour
¼ cup (35g) self-raising flour
RICOTTA FILLING
1kg ricotta cheese
1 tablespoon finely grated lemon rind
¼ cup (60ml) lemon juice
1 cup (220g) caster sugar
5 eggs
¼ cup (40g) sultanas
¼ cup (80g) finely chopped glacé fruit salad

1 Grease 28cm springform tin.
2 Beat butter, sugar and egg in small bowl with electric mixer until combined. Stir in half the sifted flours, then work in remaining flours by hand. Lightly knead pastry on floured surface until smooth; wrap in plastic; refrigerate 30 minutes.
3 Press pastry over base of tin; prick with fork. Place on oven tray; refrigerate 30 minutes.
4 Preheat oven to 200°C/180°C fan-forced.
5 Cover pastry with baking paper, fill with beans or rice; bake 10 minutes. Remove paper and beans; bake 15 minutes or until browned lightly. Cool. Reduce oven temperature to 160°C/140°C fan-forced.
6 Meanwhile, make ricotta filling.
7 Pour filling into tin; bake about 50 minutes. Cool cheesecake in oven with door ajar.
8 Refrigerate cheesecake 3 hours or overnight. Serve cheesecake dusted with sifted icing sugar, if desired.
RICOTTA FILLING Process cheese, rind, juice, sugar and eggs until smooth; stir in fruit.

{**prep + cook time** 1 hour 40 minutes (plus refrigeration & cooling time) **serves** 16}

new york cheesecake

250g plain sweet biscuits
125g butter, melted
CREAM CHEESE FILLING
750g cream cheese, softened
2 teaspoons finely grated orange rind
1 teaspoon finely grated lemon rind
1 cup (220g) caster sugar
3 eggs
¾ cup (180g) sour cream
¼ cup (60ml) lemon juice
SOUR CREAM TOPPING
1 cup (240g) sour cream
2 tablespoons caster sugar
2 teaspoons lemon juice

1 Process biscuits until fine. Add butter, process until combined. Press mixture over base and side of 24cm springform tin. Place tin on oven tray; refrigerate 30 minutes.
2 Preheat oven to 180°C/160°C fan-forced.
3 Meanwhile make cream cheese filling.
4 Pour filling into tin; bake 1¼ hours. Remove from oven; cool 15 minutes.
5 Meanwhile make sour cream topping. Spread topping over cheesecake. Bake 20 minutes. Cool in oven with door ajar.

6 Refrigerate cheesecake 3 hours or overnight.
CREAM CHEESE FILLING Beat cheese, rinds and sugar in medium bowl with electric mixer until smooth. Beat in eggs, one at a time, then sour cream and juice.
SOUR CREAM TOPPING Combine ingredients in small bowl.

{**prep + cook time** 2 hours (plus refrigeration & cooling time) **serves** 12}

brandied apricot chocolate cake

125g dark eating chocolate, chopped
½ cup (125ml) water
125g butter, softened
1 cup (220g) firmly packed brown sugar
2 eggs
½ cup (125ml) sour cream
1⅓ cups (200g) plain flour
⅓ cup (35g) self-raising flour
¼ cup (80g) apricot jam
1 tablespoon brandy
½ cup (125ml) thickened cream, whipped
CHOCOLATE ICING
90g dark eating chocolate, chopped
15g butter, chopped

1 Preheat oven to 160°C/140°C fan-forced. Grease deep 20cm-round cake pan; line base with baking paper.
2 Stir chocolate and the water in small saucepan, over low heat, until smooth; cool chocolate mixture.
3 Cream butter and sugar in small bowl with electric mixer until light and fluffy. Beat in eggs, one at a time. Transfer mixture to large bowl, stir in chocolate mixture, sour cream and sifted flours in two batches.
4 Spread mixture into pan; bake about 1 hour. Stand cake in pan 5 minutes before turning, top-side up, onto wire rack to cool.
5 Meanwhile make chocolate icing.
6 Split cake in half. Combine jam and brandy. Sandwich cake with jam mixture and cream. Spread cake with icing, refrigerate until set.
CHOCOLATE ICING Stir chocolate and butter in small bowl over small saucepan of simmering water until smooth (do not allow water to touch base of bowl); cool.

{**prep + cook time** 1 hour 20 minutes (plus refrigeration time) **serves** 10}

torta di mamma

280g packet sponge cake mix
1 cup (250ml) strong black coffee
⅓ cup (80ml) coffee liqueur
⅓ cup (80ml) brandy
1 tablespoon caster sugar
CUSTARD FILLING
½ cup (75g) cornflour
½ cup (60g) custard powder
½ cup (110g) caster sugar
2½ cups (625ml) milk
1½ cups (375ml) cream
2 teaspoons vanilla extract
30g butter
2 egg yolks
90g dark eating chocolate, melted

1 Preheat oven to 160°C/140°C fan-forced. Grease deep 22cm-round cake pan; line base with baking paper.
2 Make sponge cake according to the directions on packet; pour mixture into pan. Bake about 35 minutes. Turn cake onto wire rack to cool.
3 Meanwhile, make custard filling.
4 Combine cold coffee, liqueur, brandy and sugar in small jug; mix well. Split cold cake into four layers. Place first layer on serving plate; brush well with coffee mixture.
5 Spread half the plain custard over cake. Top custard with second layer of cake; brush with coffee mixture. Spread a third of the chocolate custard over cake. Place third layer of cake on top of custard; brush with coffee mixture then spread with remaining plain custard. Top with fourth layer of cake; brush with coffee mixture.
6 Using a large spatula, spread remaining chocolate custard over top and side of cake; refrigerate 3 hours or overnight.
CUSTARD FILLING Combine cornflour, custard powder and sugar in medium saucepan. Gradually add combined milk, cream and extract; stir over low heat until mixture boils and thickens. Add butter; simmer, stirring, 3 minutes. Remove pan from heat; stir in egg yolk. Place custard in large bowl; cover with plastic wrap. Cool. Divide custard mixture between two bowls. Stir melted chocolate into one bowl. Leave remaining custard plain.

{**prep + cook time** 1 hour 50 minutes (plus refrigeration time) **serves** 12}

rich mocha gâteau

½ cup (125ml) Cointreau
2 teaspoons finely grated orange rind
150g milk chocolate, melted
90g unsalted butter, melted
6 eggs, separated
¾ cup (110g) self-raising flour
⅓ cup (75g) caster sugar
RICH MOCHA FILLING
2 teaspoons instant coffee granules
2 tablespoons hot water
300g dark eating chocolate, melted
6 egg yolks
CHOCOLATE BUTTER CREAM
2 tablespoons instant coffee granules
¼ cup (60ml) hot water
200g dark eating chocolate, melted
4 egg yolks
¼ cup (55g) caster sugar
185g unsalted butter, softened

1 Preheat oven to 180°C/160°C fan-forced. Grease deep 22cm-round cake pan; line base with baking paper.
2 Stand liqueur and rind in small bowl for 30 minutes. Strain; reserve rind and liqueur separately.
3 Combine chocolate, butter and rind in large bowl. Stir in 3 teaspoons of the liqueur, egg yolks and sifted flour.
4 Beat egg whites in large bowl with electric mixer until soft peaks form; gradually add sugar, beating until dissolved between additions. Fold whites into chocolate mixture, in two batches.
5 Pour mixture into pan; bake about 35 minutes. Stand cake in pan 5 minutes before turning, top-side up, onto wire rack to cool.
6 Meanwhile, make rich mocha filling and chocolate butter cream.

7 Split cake into three layers. Place first layer on serving plate; spread with half the mocha filling. Refrigerate 15 minutes. Top with second layer; spread with remaining mocha filling. Top with third layer; refrigerate 30 minutes. Spread butter cream over top and side of cake; refrigerate 30 minutes.
RICH MOCHA FILLING Combine coffee and the water in large bowl; stir in melted chocolate, then yolks and ⅓ cup of the remaining liqueur. Refrigerate until set.
CHOCOLATE BUTTER CREAM Combine coffee and the water in large bowl; stir in the chocolate and remaining liqueur. Beat yolks and sugar in small bowl with electric mixer until thick and creamy; beat in butter in several batches until smooth. Gradually beat in chocolate mixture; refrigerate 10 minutes or until spreadable.

{ **prep + cook time** 1 hour 15 minutes (plus standing & refrigeration time) **serves** 12 }

chocolate mocha dacquoise terrine

4 egg whites
1 cup (220g) caster sugar
2 tablespoons cocoa powder
200g dark eating chocolate, chopped
¾ cup (180ml) cream
2 teaspoons cocoa powder, extra
MOCHA BUTTER CREAM
1 tablespoon instant coffee granules
2 tablespoons boiling water
100g unsalted butter, softened
2¼ cups (360g) icing sugar

1 Preheat oven to 150°C/130°C fan-forced. Line three oven trays with baking paper; draw a 10cm x 25cm rectangle on each sheet of baking paper.
2 Beat egg whites in medium bowl with electric mixer until soft peaks form. Gradually add sugar, beating until sugar dissolves between additions; fold in sifted cocoa.
3 Spread meringue mixture evenly over rectangles; bake about 45 minutes. Turn off oven; cool meringues in oven with door ajar.
4 Meanwhile, stir chocolate and cream in small saucepan, over low heat, until smooth, transfer to small bowl; refrigerate until firm. Beat chocolate mixture with electric mixer about 20 seconds or until just changed in colour.

5 Make mocha butter cream.
6 Place one meringue layer on serving plate; spread with half the chocolate mixture, then top with half the butter cream. Top with another meringue layer; spread with remaining chocolate mixture then remaining butter cream. Top with last meringue layer; cover and refrigerate 3 hours or overnight. Dust with sifted extra cocoa powder to serve.
MOCHA BUTTER CREAM Dissolve coffee granules in the boiling water in small bowl; cool 10 minutes. Beat butter in small bowl with electric mixer until pale in colour; gradually add sifted icing sugar, beating until combined. Beat in coffee mixture.

{**prep + cook time** 1 hour 10 minutes (plus cooling & refrigeration time) **serves** 12}

plum & almond upside-down cake

50g butter, chopped
½ cup (110g) firmly packed brown sugar
12 small plums (900g), halved, stones removed
125g butter, softened
1 teaspoon vanilla extract
1¼ cups (275g) caster sugar
3 eggs
¾ cup (110g) self-raising flour
¾ cup (110g) plain flour
¾ cup (180ml) milk
1 cup (120g) almond meal
⅓ cup (25g) flaked almonds, toasted

1 Preheat oven to 180°C/160°C fan-forced. Grease 19cm-square cake pan; line with baking paper.
2 Combine butter and brown sugar in a small saucepan, stir over low heat until smooth; pour into base of cake pan. Place plums, cut side down, over caramel mixture.
3 Beat butter, extract and caster sugar in medium bowl with electric mixer until light and fluffy. Beat in eggs, one at a time. Stir in sifted flours, and milk, in two batches. Stir in almond meal.
4 Spread mixture into pan; bake about 50 minutes. Stand cake in pan 15 minutes before turning onto wire rack to cool. Serve sprinkled with flaked almonds.

{ **prep + cook time** 1 hour 15 minutes **serves** 9 }

banana caramel layer cake

You need two large overripe bananas (460g) for this recipe.

185g butter, softened
1¼ cup (175g) caster sugar
3 eggs
2¼ cups (335g) self-raising flour
½ teaspoon bicarbonate of soda
1¼ cups mashed banana
⅓ cup (80ml) milk
380g can caramel Top 'n' Fill
¾ cup (180ml) thickened cream, whipped
1 large (230g) banana, sliced thinly

1 Preheat oven to 180°C/160°C fan-forced. Grease 24cm bundt pan or 24cm patterned silicone pan well.
2 Beat butter and sugar in small bowl with electric mixer until light and fluffy. Beat in eggs, one at a time. Transfer mixture to large bowl; stir in sifted dry ingredients, mashed banana and milk.
3 Spread mixture into pan; bake about 40 minutes. Stand cake in pan 5 minutes before turning onto wire rack to cool.
4 Split cake into three layers. Spread bottom layer of cake with half the caramel, top with half the cream then half the banana slices. Repeat next layer using remaining caramel, cream and banana slices. Replace top of cake. Dust with icing sugar before serving.

{**prep + cook time** 1 hour 10 minutes **serves** 8}

Equipment

In recent times there have been enormous changes in the cake pan market. The materials, sizes and depths have all changed but, worst of all, the sides of a lot of the new pans are now sloping, so the capacity of the pans has diminished slightly. As a baker, I find this frustrating, I'm very fond of my old "unsealed" aluminium cake pans; the cakes baked in them brown well and cook through evenly, all without developing a heavy crust. Since this book is one full of classic cakes, we decided to keep using the old faithful cake pans of yesteryear, and just hope that you still have them. My best advice is to buy up any of the old pans, there might still be some old stock around in various shops, or you might find them in second-hand shops, at fêtes or garage sales. Maybe someone in your family has some tucked away at the back of a cupboard, just looking for a loving home like yours.

If all else fails, buy new pans, buy the best you can afford; if you care for them properly they should last a lifetime. Most of the new pans have a non-stick coating, which, in my opinion, still needs a light greasing; if the surface is scratched, then the cake will definitely stick to the ungreased surface. If in doubt about any scratches, grease the pan lightly – either with butter or cooking-oil spray – then line it with baking paper. There is no need to grease the baking paper, but if the pan is greased first it makes fitting the paper inside the pan easier.

Silicone pans are now available, too, and the cakes simply fall out of them, perfect every time, but they don't develop the same crust – it's lighter – than cakes baked in aluminium pans. Supermarkets carry a vast range of inexpensive cake pans, particularly muffin, patty, friand pans etc., these will serve you well for a while, but they scratch easily – you get what you pay for with cake pans.

If you're using the non-stick coated pans, reduce the oven temperature we suggest in this book by 10°C, this will give you a better, less crusty result, and the cake will bake through very close to our suggested baking time. Make notes next to the recipe about any changes to times and temperatures you make when using these pans. My biggest concern is the capacity of the new pans, for example, the "old" deep 20cm-round cake pan, probably the most commonly used cake pan of all, will hold more cake mixture than any of the new 20cm-round pans. As a very rough guide, fill the "new" cake pan to two-thirds to three-quarters full for most butter and light fruit cakes, and about half-full for sponge mixtures. Rich fruit cakes will be fine, as they don't expand much during baking.

This is a wonderful book full of old favourite cake recipes and, with a little practice, you'll soon master the "new" cake pans.
Pamela Clark
AWW Test Kitchen Food Director

1 deep square cake pans 2 deep round cake pans 3 springform tin 4 baking dish 5 baba pan
6 angel food cake pan 7 swiss roll pan 8 loaf pan 9 bar cake pan 10 shallow round-based patty pan
11 muffin pan 12 texas muffin pan 13 dariole moulds 14 fluted ring or baba pan 15 silicone ring pan
16 mini muffin pan 17 friand pan 18 mini loaf pan 19 lamington pan 20 slice pan 21 nut roll tin

Baking techniques

There is a lot to know about baking, after all, it's all about chemistry and science. You don't need lots of fancy equipment, but you do need a reliable oven, an electric mixer for some recipes, a set of proper measuring spoons and cups, some bowls, wooden spoons and cake pans. If you're new to baking, carefully read page 226, about the old and new equipment, and then read the next few pages – this is important to ensure success and to give you confidence. Follow the recipes carefully, check the oven shelves are in the right position before you preheat the oven, and away you go.

MARBLING For a marbled effect in a cake (or frosting), dollop the various coloured mixtures into the cake pan (or on top of the cake), then pull a skewer through the mixtures.

Greasing & flouring pans

{ Cake pans need greasing, even non-stick surfaces need a light greasing. You can use cooking-oil spray, or melted butter or margarine. Use a pastry brush to grease the pans evenly. Sprinkle a little flour into the pan, shake, tap and then turn the pan until the surface is evenly floured. Tap the pan, upside-down, to get rid of the excess flour. }

Testing cakes

USE A SKEWER TO TEST MOST CAKES (NOT SPONGES OR FRUIT CAKES). TAKE THE CAKE OUT OF THE OVEN, CLOSE THE OVEN DOOR, PUSH A SKEWER GENTLY THROUGH THE THICKEST PART OF THE CAKE TO THE BOTTOM OF THE PAN. PULL THE SKEWER OUT SLOWLY: IF THE SKEWER IS CLEAN THE CAKE IS DONE; IF THE SKEWER HAS UNCOOKED MIXTURE ON IT, COOK THE CAKE FURTHER.

✱ **COOLING CAKES** Most cakes are turned out of their pans (after a specified standing time) onto wire racks to cool. Sponges are always turned out of their pans as soon as they are cooked onto a baking-paper-covered wire rack. Rich fruit cakes are usually cooled, covered tightly, in their pans.

✱ **INVERTING CAKES**
Place another wire rack on top of the cake, sandwiching the cake between the racks, then turn the cake the right way up.

✱ **SYRUPING CAKES**
Syrup cakes almost always have hot syrup poured over them when they're hot. Sometimes the syrup is poured over them while they're still in their cake pans, sometimes the cakes are turned out. In this case, the wire rack has a tray placed under it to catch the drips of syrup. This overflow should be poured back over the cake.

Lining round cake pans

Grease the cake pan evenly with either cooking-oil spray or melted butter or margarine. The greasing will ensure that the cake turns out of the pan nicely, also, it will hold the lining paper in place.

Use the base of the pan as a guide to trace around the pan onto the lining paper (use either baking or greaseproof paper). Cut out the shape, slightly inside the tracing.

Cut a strip of paper long enough to cover the side of the pan in one piece, and overlap a little at the ends. Fruit cakes need more than one layer of lining paper and the strip needs to be wide enough to cover the side, plus about 2cm for the base, plus about 5cm to extend the paper above the side of the pan.

Make a fold about 2cm wide, along one of the long sides of the strip of paper. Snip along the strip, up to the fold, at about 2cm intervals.

Position the long strip of paper around the inside of the pan. Position the base-lining paper in the pan. This method of lining a cake pan, usually with two or three layers of paper, acts as insulation during long slow baking.

LINING LAMINGTON OR BAR PANS

Cut a strip of baking or greaseproof paper long enough to cover the base and sides of the pan, and long enough to give you some paper to hold, if needing to lift the cake from the pan. The recipes will tell you to line the pan lengthways, crossways or both.

Rolling roulades & swiss rolls

The most common method is to turn the cake from the pan, trim all sides, roll the hot cake loosely with (sugared) paper, unroll, then re-roll it without the paper, cool; unroll, fill it, then re-roll it. Another method is to cool the hot cake flat before filling and rolling. Another method is to roll the trimmed hot cake, unroll it, and cool it flat before filling.

LINING SQUARE CAKE PANS

Cut strips of baking or greaseproof paper long enough to cover the base and sides of the pan, and long enough to give you some paper to hold, in case you need to lift the cake from the pan. Mostly, the pans are greased before they're lined, this method is usually used when mixtures are very wet or sticky.

Paper piping bag

* Cut a square of baking or greaseproof paper in half diagonally: be fussy about cutting the paper neatly and cleanly with sharp scissors. Hold the triangle of paper so the apex is pointing towards you, fold one corner over and around to form a cone, then fold the other corner over and around to finish the cone.

* Make sure the three points of the triangle are together, and the two sides of the paper are aligned as straight as possible. If you've made a good bag, you should not be able to see through it at the pointy end. Wriggle the paper around until it's all straight.

* Fold a little of the top of the bag over to hold the points together, then staple it; this is the best way to hold the bag together. Half-fill the bag with icing, cream, melted chocolate etc., fold the top of the bag over to enclose the icing. Use sharp scissors to snip a tiny hole at the pointy end, you can always make the hole bigger if you need to.

Egg whites

* To beat egg whites, the beaters and bowl must be clean and dry; whites will not beat up if they're in touch with fat or oil. Use a deep, not wide, bowl so the beaters can get down into the whites to create volume. Start beating on a low speed, gradually increasing the speed as the whites thicken to the correct stage for the recipe.

* Egg whites used for friands must not be beaten too much at all; use a whisk, or a fork, it doesn't really matter. The important thing is not to beat air into the whites, they simply need to be broken up evenly. Air only creates pockets, bubbles and tunnels in the dense friand mixture.

Folding-in egg whites

* This is a skill you must learn if you're going to become a good baker. It can be tricky when folding whites into a heavy mixture (such as chocolate or cake batter), or a lot of mixture. To loosen such mixtures, fold about a quarter of the whites through, using a spatula or whisk, then fold the remaining whites through in batches.

* The action of folding means that you have to pull the ingredients together in such a way that you keep the air in the mixture. We prefer to use a rubber spatula for this, as you can scrape the side of the bowl, as you fold the ingredients together.

CANDY → THERMOMETER

TO USE A CANDY THERMOMETER CORRECTLY, PUT IT IN A SMALL SAUCEPAN OF COLD WATER AND BRING IT TO THE BOIL. WHEN THE SYRUP BEGINS TO BOIL, PUT THE THERMOMETER IN THE SYRUP; LEAVE IT THERE UNTIL THE CORRECT TEMPERATURE IS REACHED THEN RETURN THE THERMOMETER TO THE PAN OF BOILING WATER, TURN OFF THE HEAT, AND COOL IN THE WATER.

Making toffee

If you're not using a candy thermometer, the water test is perfect. Before you test the toffee, remove it from the heat and let the bubbles subside completely. Drop about a teaspoon of the hot toffee into a glass of tap-cold water, it will set immediately it touches the water. There are different stages, the first stage is called "small crack", then it goes to "hard crack", and, of course, there are stages in between. The important thing is to make sure the toffee will set enough for your needs. Take the toffee out of the water, and snap it with your fingers; if you want the toffee even harder, return it to the heat and boil it some more. It won't take long to become darker and harder – allow for the fact that it will continue to cook, even after it comes off the heat, while the bubbles subside.

Sugar syrup

Sugar syrup can be used as is, or caramelised to various strengths and colours by further boiling. Add sugar and the water to a heavy-based pan, stir over high heat, without boiling, until sugar is dissolved. Use a brush dipped in water to brush grains from side of pan. When sugar is dissolved, boil, without stirring, until the correct temperature is reached.

Chocolate

Chocolate must be melted carefully and gently. This method is the safest: place a heatproof bowl (preferably glass or china) containing the roughly chopped chocolate, over a pan of barely simmering water. The water mustn't touch the bottom of the bowl. Stir chocolate occasionally until smooth, remove from the pan as soon as it's melted.

SIMPLE CHOCOLATE CURLS

Spread melted chocolate evenly over a cold surface, such as a flat oven tray, a laminated chopping board or, best of all, marble. Leave to almost set at room temperature. There are many ways of making curls. Using a melon baller, drag the baller smoothly and evenly across the surface of the chocolate. Remember, you can always re-melt your mistakes.

The simplest of all chocolate-curl making is done with a vegetable peeler. You will only be able to make small curls, but they're quick and easy, and you can curl the chocolate straight onto the surface of the cake. Use a large bar or piece of chocolate, at room temperature, and drag the peeler along the side of the bar.

GANACHE

Ganache is mostly used for frosting or filling, but it can also be used as a coating; in this case, the mixture is cooled but used before it thickens. When it's used as a frosting or filling, the ganache is cooled, sometimes in the fridge, and given an occasional stir with a wooden spoon to mix the ingredients. It can also be whipped after it has been refrigerated.

RICH FRUIT CAKE

It's important to line the cake pan properly for a good shaped cake, also, the lining paper protects the cake during the long slow cooking time. We use one or two sheets of brown paper, and two or three sheets of baking or greaseproof paper. See page 230 for how to line a round cake pan – use this same method for square pans, too. Push large spoonfuls (or handfuls) of the cake mixture into the corners of the pan to hold the paper firmly in position – this also helps to minimise air bubbles. When all the mixture is in the pan, level it with your hand or spoon, then drop the pan from about a height of 20cm onto the bench to settle the mixture into the pan.

Use a wet spatula to level the top of the mixture as evenly as you can. If you want to decorate the top of the cake with nuts or cherries etc., do it now, before you bake the cake.

Splitting & layering cakes

No need to worry about splitting and layering cakes any more, these tips will help you perfect the technique.

✱ Use a sharp serrated knife to split a cake into layers. This is quite easy to do if the cake is firm, but if it's soft, use either of the next two suggested methods for better results.

✱ Bamboo skewers are good to use as a guide for the knife as you split the cake. If the cake is large, long skewers can be pushed through the cake, from one side to the other. If the cake is small, use toothpicks to mark the layer. Use a sharp serrated knife to split the cake. Cut the cake barely above the bamboo skewers or toothpicks, you should feel the knife touch the skewers as you cut through the cake.

✱ Splitting with cotton: This method is quick, neat and efficient. Use a length (enough to hold both ends as you cut through the cake) of strong cotton or dental floss, pull the cotton firmly through the cake towards you.

Butter cake basics

MOST CAKES MADE IN A HOME KITCHEN ARE BUTTER CAKES OF SOME SORT.
THESE HELPFUL TIPS WILL ENSURE YOU GET A PERFECT CAKE EVERY TIME.

BUTTER should be soft, not melted. Have the butter at room temperature and chop it coarsely into an appropriate-sized bowl. If the kitchen is cold, stand the bowl in warm water for a while. If you forget to take the butter out of the fridge, grate it into an appropriate-sized mixing bowl, using the coarsest side of the grater. If you heat the grater under hot water then dry it well, the butter will slip off the grater easily.

Adding the extras

If adding grated citrus rind, essence or extract, beat the flavouring with the butter. The butter will "hold" the flavouring from the mixing stage through to eating. →

BEATING THE MIXTURE

BEAT THE BUTTER (AND FLAVOURING) UNTIL IT IS PALE IN COLOUR. THE BOWL NEEDS TO BE OF A SIZE AND SHAPE THAT WILL LET THE BEATERS WORK IN THE BUTTER. A DEEP, NARROW BOWL IS BETTER THAN A WIDE SHALLOW BOWL.

Eggs

should be at room temperature. Beat the first egg into the butter/sugar mix only until it is absorbed, then beat in the remaining eggs, one at a time, only until they are absorbed – over-beating will cause curdling. Some mixtures have more egg content than the butter/sugar mixture can absorb, these mixtures will curdle – don't worry. Stop beating, as the mixture will only curdle more, and continue with the recipe.

Transfer

the butter/sugar/ egg mix to a wider bowl, as it will be easier and more efficient to mix in the remaining ingredients. If making a small cake, the small bowl will often be large enough to mix in the remaining ingredients. Mostly we sift half the dry ingredients over the butter/sugar/egg mix in the larger mixing bowl, then add half the liquid. For really large mixtures, we might advise you to add the ingredients in more than two batches. When making a small cake, we might advise you to add all the dry ingredients and liquid at once. We will advise you what to do in our recipes.

sugar Once the butter is soft and creamy in colour, add all the sugar to the bowl. Caster sugar is finer than regular white crystal sugar, and will give a finer-textured cake, but one can be substituted for the other. Beat the mixture until light and fluffy. Don't try and dissolve the sugar in the butter, as this will break the butter down and cause a heavy layer at the bottom of the cake.

Flour & liquid

Usually a wooden spoon is best for mixing butter cakes at this stage. There is no need to beat the mixture, just stir the wet and dry ingredients together until everything is evenly mixed. You can do this stage with an electric mixer, but do it on a low speed, and only until the ingredients are mixed, over-beating will toughen the cake.

Once you've stirred the ingredients together until they're evenly mixed, you'll see the mixture looks a bit lumpy and coarse, so give it a beating until it changes from a coarse to a finer texture. This can be done with an electric mixer, but avoid over-beating.

INTO THE PAN Dollop spoonfuls of mixture into the pan, spread the mixture evenly to the side(s) of the pan, then tap the pan firmly on the bench to break any large air bubbles. Smooth the surface with a spatula then bake as directed in the recipe.

Glossary

ALMOND MEAL also known as ground almonds; nuts powdered to a coarse flour-like texture.
vienna almonds are toffee-coated almonds available from selected supermarkets, nut stands and gourmet food and specialty confectionery stores.

BICARBONATE OF SODA also known as baking or carb soda.

BISCUITS, PLAIN SWEET also known as cookies; a crisp sweet biscuit without icing or filling.

BUTTER use salted or unsalted (sweet) butter; 125g is equal to one stick (4 ounces) of butter.

BUTTERMILK originally the term given to the slightly sour liquid left after butter was churned from cream, today it is made similarly to yogurt. Sold alongside all fresh milk products in supermarkets; despite the implication of its name, it is low in fat.

CARAMEL TOP 'N' FILL a caramel filling made from milk and cane sugar. Can be used straight from the can for cheesecakes, slices and tarts. Has similar qualities to sweetened condensed milk, only a thicker, caramel consistency; great to use in caramel desserts.

CHOCOLATE
choc Bits also known as chocolate chips or chocolate morsels; comes in milk, white and dark chocolate varieties. Contains an emulsifier, so hold their shape in baking and are ideal for decorating.
dark eating made of cocoa liquor, cocoa butter and sugar.

freckles chocolate discs covered with hundreds and thousands.
milk eating most popular eating chocolate, mild and very sweet; similar in make-up to dark eating chocolate, with the difference being the addition of milk solids.

COCOA POWDER also known as cocoa; dried, unsweetened, roasted then ground cocoa beans.

COCONUT
desiccated dried, unsweetened, finely shredded coconut.
essence produced from coconut flavouring, oil and alcohol.
flaked dried, flaked coconut flesh.
shredded strips of dried coconut.

COFFEE LIQUEUR we use Kahlúa or Tia Maria, but you can use your favourite brand.

COINTREAU a citrus-flavoured liqueur based on oranges. You can use your favourite brand.

CORNFLOUR also known as cornstarch; used as a thickening agent. Available as 100% maize (corn) and wheaten cornflour.

CREAM CHEESE also known as Philadelphia or Philly, a soft cows-milk cheese. Also available as spreadable light cream cheese – a blend of cottage and cream cheeses. Sold in supermarkets.

CREAM OF TARTAR the acid ingredient in baking powder; added to confectionery mixtures to help prevent sugar from crystallising. Keeps frostings creamy and improves volume when beating egg whites.

CREAM we used fresh cream, unless otherwise stated. Also known as pure cream and pouring cream; has no additives unlike commercially thickened cream. Minimum fat content 35%.
sour thick commercially-cultured soured cream. Minimum fat content 35%.
thick we used thick cream with 48% fat content.
thickened a whipping cream containing a thickener. Minimum fat content 35%.

CURRANTS, DRIED tiny, almost black raisins so-named after a grape variety that originated in Corinth, Greece.

CUSTARD POWDER instant mixture used to make pouring custard; similar to North American instant pudding mixes.

FLOUR
plain an all-purpose flour made from wheat.
self-raising plain flour sifted with baking powder in the proportion of 1 cup flour to 2 teaspoons baking powder.
wholemeal flours milled from the whole wheat grain (bran, germ and flour). Available in both plain and self-raising varieties.

GINGER WINE (green ginger wine) a beverage that is 14% alcohol by volume and has the taste of fresh ginger. You can substitute it with dry (white) vermouth, if you prefer. The character of the ginger is drawn out by infusing it in spirit for an extended period.

GOLDEN SYRUP a by-product of refined sugarcane; pure maple syrup or honey can be substituted.

HAZELNUTS also known as filberts; plump, grape-sized, rich, sweet nut.
meal known as ground hazelnuts.

HUNDREDS & THOUSANDS nonpareils; tiny sugar-syrup-coated sugar crystals that come in many bright colours. Used to decorate cakes and party foods.

JAM also known as preserve or conserve; usually made from fruit.

JELLY CRYSTALS a powdered mixture of gelatine, sweetener, and artificial fruit flavouring that's used to make a moulded, translucent, quivering dessert. Also known as jello.

KIRSCH cherry-flavoured liqueur.

LEMON BUTTER also known as lemon cheese or lemon spread; a smooth spread, usually made from lemons, butter and eggs.

LOLLIES confectionery; also known as sweets or candy.

MAPLE SYRUP a thin syrup distilled from the sap of the maple tree. Maple-flavoured syrup or pancake syrup is not an adequate substitute for the real thing.

MARMALADE a preserve, usually based on citrus fruit.

MARSALA a sweet, fortified wine.

MIXED DRIED FRUIT a mix of sultanas, raisins, currants, mixed peel and cherries.

MIXED PEEL candied citrus peel.

MIXED SPICE a blend of ground spices usually consisting of cinnamon, allspice and nutmeg.

NUTS, HOW TO ROAST place shelled, peeled nuts, in a single layer, on oven tray, roast in moderate oven 8-10 minutes. Be careful to avoid burning nuts.

POPPY SEEDS tiny black seeds with a pungent flavour; store in an airtight container in a cool place or freezer.

RAISINS dried sweet grapes.

RHUBARB only eat its thick, celery-like stalks, as the leaves contain a toxic substance.

SEMOLINA made from durum wheat; milled into either fine or coarse granules.

SUGAR
brown soft, finely granulated sugar retaining molasses for its characteristic colour and flavour.
caster also known as superfine or finely granulated table sugar.
demerara a rich, golden-coloured small-grained crystal sugar having a subtle molasses flavour.
icing sugar also known as confectioners' sugar or powdered sugar; granulated sugar crushed together with a small amount of added cornflour.
raw natural light-brown coloured granulated sugar with a honey-like taste.
white a coarse, granulated table sugar, also known as crystal sugar.

SULTANAS dried grapes, also known as golden raisins.

SWEET SHERRY fortified wine.

TANGELO an orange-coloured loose-skinned, juicy, sweetly-tart citrus fruit with few seeds.

TREACLE thick, dark syrup not unlike molasses; a by-product of sugar refining.

VANILLA
bean dried long, thin pod from a tropical golden orchid; the minuscule black seeds inside the bean are used to impart a luscious vanilla flavour in baking and desserts. A whole bean can be placed in the sugar container to make the vanilla sugar often called for in recipes.
extract made by pulping chopped vanilla beans with a mixture of alcohol and water. This gives a very strong solution, and only a couple of drops are needed to flavour most dishes.
paste made from vanilla pods and contains real seeds. It is highly concentrated and 1 teaspoon replaces a whole vanilla pod without mess or fuss as you neither have to split or scrape the pod. It is found in the baking aisle of many supermarkets.

YEAST a 7g (¼oz) sachet of dried yeast (2 teaspoons) is equal to 15g (½oz) compressed yeast if substituting one for the other.

YOGURT we used unflavoured plain yogurt unless specified.

ZUCCHINI also known as courgette; small green, yellow or white vegetable belonging to the squash family.

Conversion chart

Measures

One Australian metric measuring cup holds approximately 250ml; one Australian metric tablespoon holds 20ml; one Australian metric teaspoon holds 5ml.

The difference between one country's measuring cups and another's is within a two- or three-teaspoon variance, and will not affect your cooking results. North America, New Zealand and the United Kingdom use a 15ml tablespoon.

All cup and spoon measurements are level. The most accurate way of measuring dry ingredients is to weigh them. When measuring liquids, use a clear glass or plastic jug with the metric markings.

We use large eggs with an average weight of 60g.

Dry measures

METRIC	IMPERIAL
15g	½oz
30g	1oz
60g	2oz
90g	3oz
125g	4oz (¼lb)
155g	5oz
185g	6oz
220g	7oz
250g	8oz (½lb)
280g	9oz
315g	10oz
345g	11oz
375g	12oz (¾lb)
410g	13oz
440g	14oz
470g	15oz
500g	16oz (1lb)
750g	24oz (1½lb)
1kg	32oz (2lb)

Liquid measures

METRIC	IMPERIAL
30ml	1 fluid oz
60ml	2 fluid oz
100ml	3 fluid oz
125ml	4 fluid oz
150ml	5 fluid oz (¼ pint/1 gill)
190ml	6 fluid oz
250ml	8 fluid oz
300ml	10 fluid oz (½ pint)
500ml	16 fluid oz
600ml	20 fluid oz (1 pint)
1000ml (1 litre)	1¾ pints

Length measures

METRIC	IMPERIAL
3mm	⅛ in
6mm	¼in
1cm	½in
2cm	¾in
2.5cm	1in
5cm	2in
6cm	2½in
8cm	3in
10cm	4in
13cm	5in
15cm	6in
18cm	7in
20cm	8in
23cm	9in
25cm	10in
28cm	11in
30cm	12in (1ft)

Oven temperatures

These oven temperatures are only a guide for conventional ovens. For fan-forced ovens, check the manufacturer's manual.

	°C (CELSIUS)	°F (FAHRENHEIT)	GAS MARK
Very slow	120	250	½
Slow	150	275-300	1-2
Moderately slow	160	325	3
Moderate	180	350-375	4-5
Moderately hot	200	400	6
Hot	220	425-450	7-8
Very hot	240	475	9

Index

General

baking techniques 228
   adding syrup to cakes 229
   butter cake basics 233
   cooling cakes 229
   flouring pans 229
   greasing pans 229
   inverting cakes 229
   lining cakes pans 230
   marbling cake mix 229
   measuring 229
   splitting and layering cakes 232
   syruping cakes 229
   testing cakes 229
cake pans
   differences between old
     and new 226
   lining 230
   types of 227
cakes, types of 7
candy thermometer 231
chocolate, using in baking 232
egg whites, using in baking 231
equipment 226
fruit cake, preparing mixture
   for baking 232
pans, see also cake pans 226-7
piping bags, paper 230
roulades & swiss rolls, rolling 230
sugar syrup, how to make 231
toffee, making 231

Recipes
A

almond & dark chocolate
   torte 205
almond and dutch
   ginger slice 137
almond and plum
   upside-down cake 222
almond butter cake 25
almond cherry cake 34
almond orange halva cake 186
almond vanilla pear cake 197
angel food cake 82
apple cake, warm, with brandy
   butterscotch sauce 193
apple custard tea cakes 134
apple streusel cake 118
apricot chocolate cake,
   brandied 214

B

banana and white chocolate
   patty cakes 33
banana butterscotch
   syrup cake 174
banana cake 110
banana cake with
   passionfruit icing 113
banana caramel layer cake 225
banana toffee
   upside-down cake 157
basic butter cake 10
berry cake, mixed, with
   vanilla bean syrup 166
berry muffins 142
black forest cake 190
boiled chocolate cake 90
boiled pineapple rum cake 150
boiled whisky fruit cake 114
brandied apricot
   chocolate cake 214
butter cake, almond 25
butter cake, basic 10
butter cake, cut & keep 18
butter cream
   brandied 105
   chocolate 218
   coffee 206
   filling 74
   mocha 221
butterfly cakes 37
buttermilk cake, chocolate 101
buttermilk cake, lime syrup 182
butterscotch banana
   syrup cake 174

C

caramel banana layer cake 225
carrot cake with lemon cream
   cheese frosting 154
cashew and maple syrup
   upside-down loaf 38
celebration fruit cake 145
cheesecake, italian ricotta 210
cheesecake, new york 213
cherry almond cake 34
chiffon cake, chocolate 105
chocolate and orange
   patty cakes 33
chocolate apricot cake,
   brandied 214
chocolate buttermilk cake 101
chocolate cake, boiled 90
chocolate cake, one-bowl 97
chocolate chiffon cake 105
chocolate cup cakes,
   fudge-frosted 106
chocolate dessert cake,
   flourless 201
chocolate fudge brownies 93
chocolate fudge cake 102
chocolate ganache 86, 205, 206
chocolate hazelnut cake,
   flourless 94
chocolate mocha dacquoise
   terrine 221
chocolate roulade with
   coffee cream 194
chocolate sponge 73
chocolate, dark, & almond
   torte 205
chocolate, white, and banana
   patty cakes 33
cinnamon and walnut syrup
   cake 181
cinnamon teacake 22
citrus poppy seed friands 141
coconut cake 42
coconut raspberry slice 138
coffee cream, chocolate
   roulade with 194
coffee walnut streusel cake 50
coulis, strawberry 201
cream cheese lemon cake 46
cream, vienna 45
cup cakes, fudge-frosted
   chocolate 106
curd, passionfruit 77
custard and apple tea cakes 134
custard filling 134, 217

D

dacquoise terrine, chocolate
   mocha 221

dark chocolate & almond
   torte 205
date and walnut rolls 129
dessert cake, flourless
   chocolate 201
devil's food cake 89
dundee cake 158
dutch ginger and almond slice 137

E

english malt loaf 30
espresso syrup cake 178

F

featherlight sponge cake 61
fillings
   butter cream 74
   chocolate 101
   cream cheese 213
   custard 134, 217
   ginger cream 58
   passionfruit curd 77
   rich mocha 218
   ricotta 210
flourless chocolate
   dessert cake 201
flourless chocolate
   hazelnut cake 94
friands, citrus poppy seed 141
frostings (see icings & frostings)
fruit and yogurt loaf 130
fruit cake, boiled whisky 114
fruit cake, celebration 145
fruit cake, glacé 185
fruit cake, last-minute 146
fruit cake, rich sherried 149
fudge brownies, chocolate 93
fudge cake, chocolate 102
fudge-frosted chocolate
   cup cakes 106

G

ganache, chocolate 86, 205, 206
gâteau, rich mocha 218
gateau, opera 206
génoise sponge 54
ginger and almond slice,
   dutch 137

ginger cake 41
ginger fluff roll 58
ginger sponge 78
gingerbread loaves 26
glaze (chocolate) 206
greek yogurt cake 29

H

hazelnut chocolate cake,
   flourless 94
honey spice sponge cake 62
hummingbird cake 121

I

icings and frostings
   brandied butter cream 105
   butter frosting 13
   chocolate icing 33, 69, 74,
     97, 98, 214
   chocolate butter cream 218
   chocolate ganache, dark 86,
     205, 206
   coconut ice frosting 42
   coffee icing 33, 73
   cream cheese frosting 121
   fudge frosting 90, 106
   glacé icing 33, 46
   lemon cream cheese
     frosting 154
   lemon frosting 41
   mocha butter cream 221
   passionfruit icing 33, 113
   rich chocolate frosting 89
   vanilla 6, 26
   vienna cream 45
italian ricotta cheesecake 210

J

jam roll 57
jelly cakes, strawberry 66

K

kisses 45

L

lamington roll 74
lamingtons 69

layer cake, banana caramel 225
lemon cream cheese cake 46
lemon sour cream cake 14
lemon syrup cake 170
lemon yogurt and semolina
   syrup cake 177
lime and passionfruit
   patty cakes 33
lime syrup buttermilk cake 182
loaf, english malt 30
loaf, one-bowl sultana 133
loaf, pecan and raisin 126
loaf, upside-down cashew and
   maple syrup 38
loaf, yogurt fruit 130
loaf, zucchini walnut 162
loaves, gingerbread 26
lumberjack cake 122

M

madeira cake 21
malt loaf, english 30
maple syrup and cashew
   upside-down loaf 38
marble cake 13
mississippi mud cake 86
mixed berry cake with
   vanilla bean syrup 166
mocha chocolate dacquoise
   terrine 221
mocha gâteau, rich 218
mocha patty cakes 33
mocha puddings,
   soft-centred 198
moist whole orange cake 125
mud cake, mississippi 86
mud cake, rich truffle 202
muffins, berry 142

N

new york cheesecake 213

O

one-bowl sultana loaf 133
opera gateau 206
orange almond halva cake 186
orange and chocolate
   patty cakes 33

orange cake 17
orange cake, moist whole 125
orange poppy seed syrup cake 169
orange syrup cake 173

P

passionfruit and lime
    patty cakes 33
passionfruit curd 77
passionfruit curd sponge cakes 77
patty cakes
    banana & white chocolate 33
    chocolate & orange 33
    mocha 33
    passionfruit & lime 33
    quick-mix patty cakes 33
pear almond vanilla cake 197
pecan and raisin loaf 126
pineapple rum cake, boiled 150
plum and almond upside-down
    cake 222
poppy seed citrus friands 141
poppy seed orange syrup cake 169
pound cake 49
powder puffs, strawberry 65
praline, walnut 105
puddings, soft-centred mocha 198

R

raisin and pecan loaf 126
raspberry coconut slice 138
rich mocha gâteau 218
rich sherried fruit cake 149
rich truffle mud cake 202
ricotta cheesecake, italian 210
rock cakes 153
roll, ginger fluff 58
roll, jam 57
roll, lamington 74
rolls, date and walnut 129
roulade, chocolate, with
    coffee cream 194
rum baba 209

S

sacher torte 98
semolina and yogurt
    lemon syrup cake 177

siena cake 161
slice, dutch ginger and
    almond 137
slice, raspberry coconut 138
sour cream cake, lemon 14
spice cake, honey sponge 62
sponge cake, honey spice 62
sponge cake, best-ever 81
sponge cake, featherlight 61
sponge cakes, passionfruit curd 77
sponge, chocolate 73
sponge, génoise 54
sponge sandwich, victoria 70
sticky date cake with
    butterscotch sauce 117
strawberry coulis 201
strawberry jelly cakes 66
strawberry powder puffs 65
streusel 118
streusel cake, apple 118
streusel coffee walnut cake 50
sultana loaf, one-bowl 133
syrup cake, banana
    butterscotch 174
syrup cake, cinnamon and
    walnut 181
syrup cake, espresso 178
syrup cake, lemon 170
syrup cake, lime buttermilk 182
syrup cake, orange 173
syrup cake, orange poppy
    seed 169
syrup cake, semolina and
    yogurt lemon 177
syrups
    butterscotch 174
    coffee 206
    espresso 178
    ginger 185
    lemon 170, 177
    lime 182
    orange 169
    orange and brandy 186
    rum 209
    sugar 181
    vanilla bean 166

T

tea cakes, apple custard 134
teacake, cinnamon 22

terrine, chocolate mocha
    dacquoise 221
toffee banana upside-down
    cake 157
toppings
    coconut 122, 138
    glaze (chocolate) 206
    sour cream 213
    streusel 118
    walnut streusel 50
torta di mamma 217
torte, dark chocolate &
    almond 205
truffle mud, cake rich 202

U

upside-down cake, plum and
    almond 222
upside-down cashew and maple
    syrup loaf 38
upside-down toffee banana
    cake 157

V

vanilla pear almond cake 197
victoria sponge sandwich 70
vienna cream 45

W

walnut and cinnamon
    syrup cake 181
walnut and date rolls 129
walnut praline 105
walnut streusel 50
walnut streusel coffee cake 50
walnut zucchini loaf 162
white chocolate and banana
    patty cakes 33

Y

yogurt cake, greek 29
yogurt fruit loaf 130
yogurt lemon and semolina
    syrup cake 177

Z

zucchini walnut loaf 162

First published in 2009 by ACP Books, Sydney
Reprinted 2009, 2011 (twice).

ACP Books are published by ACP Magazines,
a division of Nine Entertainment Co.

ACP Books

General manager Christine Whiston
Editor-in-chief Susan Tomnay
Creative director Hieu Chi Nguyen
Art director & designer Hannah Blackmore
Senior editor Wendy Bryant
Food director Pamela Clark
Food editor Rebecca Squadrito
Project food editor Cathie Lonnie
Sales & rights director Brian Cearnes
Marketing manager Bridget Cody
Senior business analyst Rebecca Varela
Operations manager David Scotto
Production manager Victoria Jefferys

Published by ACP Books, a division of ACP Magazines Ltd,
54 Park St, Sydney; GPO Box 4088, Sydney, NSW 2001.
phone (02) 9282 8618 fax (02) 9126 3702.
acpbooks@acpmagazines.com.au
www.acpbooks.com.au

Printed by C&C Offset Printing, China.

Australia Distributed by Network Services,
phone +61 2 9282 8777; fax +61 2 9264 3278;
networkweb@networkservicescompany.com.au
New Zealand Distributed by Southern Publishers Group,
phone (64 9) 360 0692; fax (64 9) 360 0695;
hub@spg.co.nz
South Africa Distributed by PSD Promotions,
phone (27 11) 392 6065/6/7; fax (27 11) 392 6079/80;
orders@psdprom.co.za

Special feature photographer Julie Crespel
Special feature stylist Lynsey Fryers
Special feature food preparation Nicole Jennings & Amal Webster

Photographers Andre Martin, Brett Stevens, Gerry Colley, Gorta Yuuki,
Ian Wallace, John Paul Urizar, Joshua Dasey, Louise Lister, Rob Palmer

Stylists Amber Keller, Julz Beresford, Kay Francis, Kirsty Cassidy,
Louise Pickford, Margot Braddon, Marie-Helene Clauzon,
Michaela Le Compte, Sarah O'Brien, Stephanie Souvlis, Yael Grinham

Title: Classic cakes / food director, Pamela Clark.
ISBN: 978-1-86396-873-7
Notes: Includes index.
Subjects: Cake.
Other Authors/Contributors: Clark, Pamela.
Also Titled: Australian women's weekly.
Dewey Number: 641.8653
© ACP Magazines Ltd 2009
ABN 18 053 273 546

The publishers would like to thank the following for props used in photography:
Empire Vintage; Essential Ingredient; Miljo (for Amapola in silver 1965_3 by Tres Tintas);
Mokum Textiles; Mud Australia; No Chintz Fabrics; Pepe's Paperie (for Elum Rococo Pink Gift wrap);
Porters Paints (for Sparrow in gold and Sparrow in blue by Catherine Martin);
South Pacific Fabrics; Top 3 By Design; Tres Fabu!; Waterford Wedgwood.

To order books, phone 136 116 (within Australia) or
order online at www.acpbooks.com.au
Send recipe enquiries to: recipeenquiries@acpmagazines.com.au